Walking a Literary Labyrinth

WALKING A LITERARY LABYRINTH

A Spirituality of Reading

NANCY M. MALONE

RIVERHEAD BOOKS

New York

RIVERHEAD BOOKS
Published by The Berkley Publishing Group
A division of Penguin Group (USA) Inc.
375 Hudson Street
New York, New York 10014

Copyright © 2003 by Nancy M. Malone
Cover art and design by Jess Morphew

A list of permissions appears on page 209.

First Riverhead hardcover edition: June 2003
First Riverhead trade paperback edition: July 2004
Riverhead trade paperback ISBN: 1-59448-002-8

The Library of Congress has catalogued the Riverhead
hardcover edition as follows:

Malone, Nancy M.
Walking a literary labyrinth : a spirituality of reading / Nancy M. Malone.
p. cm.
ISBN 1-57322-246-1 (acid-free paper)
1. Books and reading.   2. Malone, Nancy M.—Books and reading.
3. Nuns—Books and reading.   4. Spiritual life.   I. Title.
Z1003.M25   2003   2003043107
028.9—dc21

Printed in the United States of America

10 9 8 7 6 5 4 3 2 1

In memory of

DORINDA ROMANINI MARAFFI,

my immigrant grandmother, a valiant woman of great faith

ACKNOWLEDGMENTS

To begin at the beginning, I wish to express my gratitude to the Louisville Institute, from which I received the grant that made it financially feasible for me to undertake the writing of this book. And to Suzanne Hoover, who believed in its possibilities from beginning to end. I am grateful as well to all those family members, sisters, and friends who supported me, encouraged me, prayed for me, helped me find quotes, and read earlier drafts—including my good neighbor, who regularly appeared at my door with hot homemade dishes, helping me keep body and soul together at those crunch times when I was living on peanut butter sandwiches.

But above all, I wish to thank my editors at Riverhead: Erin Moore, whose first careful readings set me on the right path; and Cindy Spiegel, who pushed, pulled, squeezed, demanded, and coaxed from me every bit of clarity and explication of which I was capable, even when I didn't know that I was. I am more grateful to them than I can say.

Contents

A Literary *Contemplatio ad Amorem*

Imagination: Faith, Hope, and Love

Epilogue

"Give Beauty Back": An Apologia

This classic eleven-circuit labyrinth reproduces the ancient design as it appears on the floor of the cathedral at Chartres, where it is thought to have served medieval Christians as a substitute for making a pilgrimage to Jerusalem. Unlike the legendary labyrinth at Crete, a maze built by Daedalus to imprison the Minotaur, there are no dead ends or blind alleys in this design. In a roundabout fashion, the path always leads to the center, and the same path is followed outward to the rim. Rediscovered as a spiritual practice in the last decade, walking the labyrinth can be used as a meditative tool in our search for wholeness, its pattern understood as symbolizing our journey through life.

PROLOGUE

HAS IT EVER occurred to you that the acts of reading and meditation resemble each other in many ways? Both are usually done alone, in silence and physical stillness, our attention focused, our whole selves—body, mind, and heart—engaged. Both can draw us deeply into ourselves, all the while taking us out of ourselves. Our consciousness shifts. We are not our everyday selves with various roles to play in our families, our jobs, society, with our concerns, major and minor, about the people we love, the things we have to do, our needs and wants, the state of the world. We become centered, our energy concentrated, with no purpose served by what we are doing other than the act itself. We are, at the moment, only the reader, or the contemplative.

These moments of wholeness, experienced sometimes in reading, sometimes in prayer, give us hints at what can be said about spirituality and reading, about a spirituality of reading. Such is the human condition, however, that even when we devote ourselves entirely to a book (or to prayer) we don't bring a completed, finished self to it. Think, for instance, of the novels that spoke to you when you were eighteen, that you regard as superficial or exaggerated now. Or think of revisiting one of the classics, only to discover a different, deeper book than the one you read decades ago. It's not the books that have changed. It is you yourself.

And some of the changes in you have been brought about by the books that you have read in the meantime. In fact, you may credit significant turns that you have taken in life to a certain book, or certain books. Less noticed by us, however, are the many more subtle ways that our reading has influenced the works-in-progress that we are, or how our reading has led us, one way or another, on the journey we've made to become who we are now. And we can be sure that, as long as we live and read, other books will accompany us, like wise and honest friends on the quest to become who we are meant to be.

It is this journey that I mean when I use the word *spirituality*. For me spirituality encompasses not only our search for a personal relationship with the divine, a Higher Power, with God—the Transcendent Other, omnipotent, eternal, in heaven, or somewhere "out there." I understand it at the same time and necessarily as the quest for "the God within," spoken of in most of the great world religions. The quest for "God in you, as you," the startling phrase I encountered in the writings of theologian John Dunne years ago. For the "true self," as Thomas Merton so often termed it.

From your own life experience, you know that the path we follow in this search doesn't lead us in straight lines directly to our goal, from A to B, or Q, or Z. It is more like the path of a labyrinth, laid out in circuits, with abrupt about-face turns and wide swings, bringing us now nearer to, now farther from the center as we move into it, now nearer to and farther from the outermost rim as we leave it. I see the labyrinth, itself a metaphor for our journey through life, as offering us a way of reflecting on the role of reading in that journey, a symbol of the part reading can play in the search for the true self.

At least that has been the pattern, the story, of my life. For me, reading—and I don't mean just inspirational, devotional reading—has been and is a spiritual practice. It is my partner in the conversation we are always having with ourselves (our interiority), influencing who I've thought I was, who I wanted to be, who I am and am called to be. As in the lives of Augustine and Ignatius of Loyola—though not so immediately—it has been a midwife at rebirths I have undergone (conversion), and it has, at times, taught me lessons about who I am not. I have found a kind of intimacy—an exchange of selves—in reading, and have been helped by it toward intimacy with myself and with God.

In one interpretation of the labyrinth, when you reach its center, you reach your true self, and then proceed outward again to communion with God and with others. Paradoxically, I have found that the deeper the journey into the self, the wider its embrace, or so it has been in my life and in my reading, in my reading life. When you find your true self and God, you find everybody. "Here comes everybody," as James Joyce said of the Catholic (catholic at its best) church. Or to put it another way, in the labyrinth, as I came to understand it, it is not the small circle at the center that symbolizes the self but the whole grand design, every experience and everyone you meet and every book that you read making you who you are—your self—the given, the goal, and with you every step along the way. And that sends you, every time you walk it, right out into the world again.

Inescapably, I have written as the Roman Catholic nun that I am. But I invite you as readers from all religious traditions, or from none, to join me, and to consider the influence of reading in your own life: on your interiority, on the turning points in your journey, on your desires for intimacy, for union and communion. And I hope that, however roundabout the path we take, I will be able to convey something of what I mean by a spirituality of reading—the search for the true self in reading, for the self that sees the world with the faith that Jesuit Bernard Lonergan calls "the eye of love."

Now, as the priest used to say at the beginning of a liturgical procession, *"Procedamus in pace,"* together. Let us proceed in peace, as we walk a literary labyrinth in this book, and, when we leave it, in the world.

THE ABCs
OF THE SELF

First Steps to Interiority

For years, I have gone every summer to the Mercy Center in Madison, Connecticut, to make my annual retreat. My motives for going there, and at this time of year, are not unmixed. Besides an astute spiritual director, thoughtfully prepared liturgies, and good healthy food, the center, located on beautifully landscaped residential shorefront property, offers me an unbroken view of the placid waters of Long Island Sound, and the opportunity for a daily swim. I love the sea, and I love to swim.

When I returned to Mercy in the summer of 1998, I was delighted to find that a labyrinth had been laid out there at the far edge of the front lawn, next to the grassy dunes that drop down to the beach. The seven-circuit design is pleasing to the eye, satisfying to look at. Stony Creek granite pebbles describe the circular path to the center, the turns and about-faces marked by inlaid bricks and low-lying shrubs. Under the dome of the sky, which meets the sea at the horizon you face, you enter the labyrinth on a straight path that takes you, before the first turning, to somewhere just short of the middle of the pattern. You begin to walk the labyrinth *in medias res,* in the middle of things, where many stories begin, where this one begins.

I live in a two-room ground-floor flat on the west side of City Island in the Bronx, only yards from the waters of Eastchester Bay. On summer days, when the tide is right and I wake up hot and sweaty, I often go—before breakfast, before my morning meditation—for a swim. I'm not an athletic swimmer; I don't do laps—just a few dozen strokes of the crawl and the breast and side strokes. I savor the feelings of buoyancy, coolness, total immersion, myself small in the whole wide bay, and when I float on my back, the sky all over me. My swim puts things—me and my life—in perspective. It's a good way to start the day.

And at night, when I've closed the door on my million-dollar view of the Manhattan skyline, the Bronx Whitestone and Throgs Neck bridges with their blue-lighted arcs, I read. I'm not a purposeful reader; I don't have a program, or make lists or notes. I read for pleasure. But I am a constant reader. And if I tell the truth, I am more likely to miss my night prayers on occasion than my reading. It is another experience of total immersion, of a world wider than mine—a good way to end the day.

It was in 1994, after forty-one years of living as a nun in religious communities large and small, and in something of a spiritual crisis, that I received permission from my religious superiors to live alone. I am still a nun, a member in good standing of the Ursuline order; I stay in close touch with my superiors and sisters. And until 1997, when I retired to try my hand at writing full-time, I served as co-editor of the interreligious journal *Cross Currents*. While not a hermit now, I have been freed from the constraints of community living and of a job; with longer periods of silence, solitude, and leisure at my disposal, I have had more time to read and to reflect on the part that reading plays in my spiritual life, and in my life as a whole.

City Island is located just over the Westchester line in the North Bronx. Although it boasts several art galleries and antique shops, Martha's Vineyard it is not. It is funky, with the oddest mixture of people—long-haired, aging hippies, bleached blondes in tights, sailors, merchants, middle-class homeowners, and the denizens of several expensive condos, on the whole not overly friendly people. One-story cottages whose yards are littered with old boats, cars, and debris stand cheek by jowl with charming white-shingled, black-shuttered houses, and brick duplexes. City Island Avenue, our sole commercial thoroughfare, features boatyards both abandoned and flourishing, and several large Italian-cum-fish restaurants. (Arthur Schwartz, reviewing one of these in the *Daily News,* said that he could only describe its decor as "Hollywood-on-the-Riviera by way of Mosholu Parkway.") Little delis and "gift shoppes" come and go.

Only a mile long and half a mile wide, the island is something like the peninsula in that section of Bridgeport, Connecticut, called Black Rock, where I was born and grew up. Our street, Lake Avenue, was bounded at one end by Ash Creek, and a block away at the other by Black Rock harbor, which lets out into Long Island Sound. Like City Island, Black Rock was and is an ethnically and economically mixed community. When I was looking for a place to live, this similarity and the water made me know that I might find a home here.

I never saw my mother read a book. Although the house my parents built several years before the crash of

1929 was beautifully furnished, thanks to her innate good taste, I have more books in my two rooms than we had in the entire house on Lake Avenue. My mother—a gifted pianist, the organist at our church for forty years, and a smart businesswoman who worked in my father's real estate and insurance company—was one of the most unreflective people I have known; she thought with her Italian blood. My second-generation Irish-American father, a sweet, small man, and witty when he was well, dropped out of high school at the death of his father. He read only those 5" × 7" detective stories with lurid covers, always reading the ending first. Two tables at either end of the living room couch held all our books in their single lower V-shaped shelves, the kind of nondescript books with tan or light blue covers scattered around inns now to make them look homey. Standing out from the others, by virtue of being larger and forbidden to me, was Radclyffe Hall's novel of lesbian love, *The Well of Loneliness,* whose pages I searched through as a teenager without being able to figure out what was forbidden about it. I couldn't tell you the titles of the other books. Maybe my mother bought them just to fill the end-table shelves.

"Usually, normatively, before reading comes being read to aloud by a parent," wrote a friend about his experience of reading. "The voice of the person, the closeness of the person, together on a couch, or the child on the lap of the reader . . . a desirable social situation . . . voice, body, indirect I-and-Thou, the love dance." There is, I believe, a kind of intimacy sought in reading (and in prayer), but I don't remember being read to as a child, and not until I was an adult did I discover children's classics like *Winnie-the-Pooh* and *The Wind in the Willows*.

My deepest childhood memory of faithful reading comes from visiting my Italian immigrant grandmother, Granny Maraffi, and seeing her absorbed in her prayer books every day after lunch. Though she taught herself to read English, the prayer books must have been in Italian. At twenty-seven, she had left her husband and two-year-old son behind to come to America alone. Family lore has it that as the boat left Genoa, she saw Grampa, little Emil in hand, walking into a tavern. They joined her later, but Grampa never really learned to speak English, much less read it.

My priest cousin and I have always thought that our vocations to religious life were rooted in Granny's deep faith. Maybe, too, the seeds of a spirituality of reading were planted as I watched her reading and praying. Like St. Augustine, who wondered at seeing St. Ambrose reading to himself—the first definite instance in Western literature of the human race passing, as every literate child does, from reading out loud to reading silently—maybe I too caught intimations of interiority in watching Granny. As Brian Stock, a professor of comparative literature, notes in *Augustine the Reader:*

> Viewing the bishop . . . [Augustine] saw something that he had apparently not seen before—the silent decoding of written signs as a means of withdrawing from the world and focusing attention on one's inner life. . . . It is the observation of a person's contemplativeness, rather than the technique of reading itself, that makes the moment unique in the ancient literature of interiority.

But we need to go back even further if we are to understand Ambrose's experience and Augustine's surprise. What made it possible for both Ambrose and my grandmother to read in this way, silently and introspectively, was that astonishing yet taken-for-granted human invention, the phonetic alphabet. The history of writing and reading, culminating in the alphabet as we know it and shared by almost all Western languages, is fascinating, complex, and long, beginning in the fourth millennium B.C.E. Reflecting on that history in *Orality and Literacy,* Jesuit polymath Walter Ong concluded that:

Writing, more than any other single invention, has transformed human consciousness. . . . By separating the knower from the known . . . writing makes possible increasingly articulate introspectivity, opening the psyche as never before not only to the external objective world quite distinct from itself but also to the interior self against whom the objective world is set.

How did, could, writing effect such a transformation? Here is a simplified account of this still-disputed process, its outline borrowed from the *Encyclopedia Americana*.

In the earliest form of writing, we humans drew pictures of things, already an abstraction from the world "out there." Then, in a transitional stage, abbreviated pictures were transformed into arbitrary symbols, at first of things and later, importantly, of sounds and words. At this point, we took another step away from the outside world and toward ourselves. We could represent now not only corn and sheep and jugs of wine, but ideas, and our own inner invisible thoughts and feelings, all the while lending words a permanence that the fleeting spoken word does not have. Finally, when phonetic writing prevailed, the sounds of words were represented at first in syllables, and later, in a further refinement, by alphabetical symbols or letters standing for the phonemes—the vowel and consonant sounds—that make up our words. Now we had a graphic counterpart of speech itself. We could represent and pass on to others in an enduring way the realities that we observed and discovered within and without for their inspection and introspection. To our point, we could express our selves and learn about the selves of others beyond the limits of time and space that constrain the spoken word.

There is a passage in Isak Dinesen's *Out of Africa* that dramatically captures the power of writing and its relationship to the self at a time when Africa itself was passing from orality to literacy. Dinesen became involved in settling a dispute among some of the indigenous people when she was asked by one of them, Jogona, to write down for him an account of his version of the story. It was a complicated matter involving degrees of kinship, property, spoken agreements, and more; it took a long time for him to remember it and get it straight, and for Dinesen to record it. When she finally was able to read the story back to him, he listened, turned away from her as if to avoid all distractions.

But as I read out his own name, "And he sent for Jogona Kanyagga, who was his friend and who lived not far away," he swiftly turned his face to me, and gave me a great fierce flaming glance, so exuberant with laughter that it changed the old man into a boy, into the very symbol of youth. Again as I had finished the document and was reading out his name, where it had figured as a verification below his thumb mark, the vital direct glance was repeated, this time deepened and calmed, with a new dignity.

Such a glance did Adam give the Lord when He formed him out of the dust, and breathed into his nostrils the breath of life, and man became a living soul. I had created him and shown him himself: Jogona Kanyagga of life everlasting. When I handed him the paper, he took it reverently and greedily folded it up in a corner of his cloak and kept his hand upon it. He could not afford to lose it, for his soul was in it, and it was the proof of his existence. Here was something which Jogona Kanyagga had performed, and which would preserve his name forever: the flesh was made word and dwelt among us full of grace and truth.

Dinesen, in highly intuitive fashion, packs a great deal into this passage: notions of the power of the written word, especially as it is experienced by the illiterate; of its ability to affirm the identity of the self (as does our signature), to confirm our existence long after the passing away of our mortal flesh.

But she does more. Instinctively reaching for religious imagery, she draws upon the book of Genesis to relate the experience of the written word to our very soul, to the creation of our selves, to our consciousness of ourselves as more than merely physical beings. Then, quoting but inverting a line from the Fourth Gospel that describes Jesus Christ as God, the Word made flesh—"And the Word became flesh and lived among us . . . full of grace and truth" (John 1:14)—she points reading and writing to the divine. It is a daring passage.

Still, Jogona *heard* the written word read to him by another, as did most people in the history that we have just traced. It took centuries before silent reading became the usual method of reading. The technologies of writing itself, from chisel and stone, to stylus and tablet, through hand-copied manuscripts, severely limited the availability of reading material. Prejudices in favor of the "living" spoken word and against the "dead" written word prevailed for a time. The skills of writing and reading were possessed by few, making the great majority of people dependent upon listening to another read. Sacred texts, in particular, were thought to be the preserve only of those divinely ordained to read them aloud for the many, thus ensuring correct interpretation.

And since, just as when we speak we don't separate the sounds of our words from one another, in an earlier stage of writing, words were not separated but written continuously; even when reading alone, one had to hear them to distinguish their meaning, as does a person learning to read now before the skill of word recognition is acquired. Conventions of punctuation, small and capital letters, paragraphs, reading from left to right, and so on, had to be established to enable understanding of the text. Thus, according to Alberto Manguel, in *The History of Reading*, it was not until the tenth century C.E. that reading silently became usual.

And thus it has come about that we read now, for the most part, silently, not giving a moment's thought to the complex process we are engaged in. But does silent reading lead us to greater interiority and introspectivity? I believe so, though it's hard to pin down exactly how. Manguel says that "with silent reading the reader was at last able to establish an unrestricted relationship with the book and the words. The words no longer needed to occupy the time required to pronounce them. They could exist in interior space . . . could echo just as well within as without." Stock, citing Augustine, speaks of the silence as a space for discovery, for interpretation, "a hermeneutic space that is emptied of outer, physical sound, so that it can be opened up to inner, permanent knowledge."

It is true that this kind of reading resembles the meditative techniques we associate with cultivation of the interior life. The words we read fix our attention. We pause over them and the thoughts they suggest, comparing them in unbroken silence with our own experience. Sometimes, as can happen in contemplative prayer, we're taken completely out of ourselves as we read, and return to ourselves refreshed. In any case, like our own interior conversation, what we read remains totally within us, all the while engaging us in conversation with another human mind, and thus subtly instructing, refining, giving form to the soliloquy that is our interiority. At least, that's what I think happens to me when I read.

Such has been the journey that the human race has taken from orality to literacy, from "the primacy of the ear to the primacy of the eye"—and to greater inwardness and the awareness of ourselves that reading brings. Ong further claims that "writing makes possible the great introspective religious traditions such as Buddhism, Judaism, Christianity, and Islam." Whether we profess belief in any of these traditions or not, surely we have inherited from them, perhaps inchoately or unconsciously—"in the recesses of the psyche," as he says—some notion of a spiritual dimension to the self, if only, for those of us in the West, because of the embeddedness of the language of the Bible in our language and literature.

Just so now, when a child learns to read, out loud at first, and then silently, she not only becomes a citizen of our literate world, she also takes a crucial step into a new kind of selfhood, and may cross the threshold into fuller participation in one of these traditions. In medieval Jewish society, according to Manguel, this step was ritually observed.

On the Feast of Shavuot, when Moses received the Torah from the hand of God, the boy about to be initiated was wrapped in a prayer shawl and taken by his father to the teacher. The teacher sat the boy on his lap and showed him a slate on which were written the Hebrew alphabet, a passage from Scriptures and the words "May the Torah be your occupation." The teacher read out every word and

the child repeated it. Then the slate was covered
with honey and the child licked it, thereby bodily
assimilating the holy words.

They were sweet to the taste: "O taste and see that the
Lord is good" (Psalm 34:8).

I experienced just such a sweet moment, though a private, silent one, not long after making my first holy communion. I was at mass, and in my little first communion
prayer book with its shiny white cover and picture of Jesus
in his red robe, I had found the perfect prayer. I don't remember anything about the prayer except that it filled my
seven-year-old heart with happiness. Mysteriously, search
though I did page by page through the book, I was never
able to find it again.

I had learned to read at St. Ann's School, a parochial
grammar school in Bridgeport, the same 1930s–40s cultur-
ally backward city left behind by the ambitious woman in
Maureen Howard's *Bridgeport Bus* (and revisited by Howard in her 1992 *Natural History*, which depicts the city in its
later condition of harrowing disintegration). At St. Ann's,
under the tutelage of the Daughters of Charity, with their
white-winged headdresses—the nuns you see in the background of a lot of period French movies—I was taught

phonics, and almost as important, perhaps, to love and care for books. We learned from the sisters how to treat new books, beginning with opening the back and front covers alternately, running our fingers down the inner spine, and proceeding with the same action, alternately back and front, in small increments of pages to the middle of the book. We learned how to cover our books and were penalized if we didn't.

Under an especially gifted seventh-grade teacher, Sister Julia, we published the 13" × 8½" *St. Ann's Echo,* a school newspaper, which we wrote and mimeographed ourselves. (Oh the toil and trouble of mimeographing, unknown to the "X-for-Xerox" generations: the hard-to-cut filmy blue stencil, the inky black drum, sometimes turned by hand, the danger of smudging, jamming . . .) And we produced a twenty-four-page yearbook, printed on glossy paper, complete with school history, class history, and class prophecy, all written by us, and photographs—of the pastor, the school building, the class of 1945, the basketball and baseball teams, and of the editorial staff and me, the editor, unsmiling so as to conceal my braces. Sister Julia's idea of a reward for good behavior was to get first dibs in choosing a new book from the shelves at the back of the room. And it was she who taught us the questions for identifying the parts of speech—who, what; which, what kind; how, when, where, why—and diagramming, so that we could fill a blackboard with Erector set–like constructions: tripods in the air for noun clauses, hanging girders for adjectival and adverbial modifiers.

I marvel at these accomplishments now. This was not, after all, some select private academy in New York City, but St. Ann's parochial school in Bridgeport, Connecticut. Maybe Sister Julia was an exception, but I am fairly sure that most of the sisters then did not have their bachelor's degrees but were earning them credit by credit over long periods of time in summer school. Yet I learned from them, from her, much of the grammar I needed to get through an MA in Latin as a young nun at Catholic University, and these same basics would stand me in good stead studying theology in a master's program at the Harvard Divinity School.

From seventh grade through high school, I had no thought of entering the convent. Like Teresa of Ávila, who, inspired by reading the lives of the martyrs when she was a little girl, started off with her brother for the country of the Moors in order to be beheaded, I too had engaged in childish acts of self-sacrifice that were born of reading. Not quite as heroic as Teresa, my friend Jean and I walked to and from school more than once with pebbles in our shoes. (I don't remember whom we were imitating; Jean says it was Little Lord Fauntleroy!) But the adult Teresa acknowledges that her motivation was suspect, that she naively reckoned martyrdom a quick and easy way to attain eternal bliss. I trudged to mass in the early-morning dark every day during Lent, not because of devotion to the eucharist or out of love for God, but because that was what you had to do to merit the rank of general on Sister Julia's "Soldiers of Christ" chart.

Soon after, I stopped raising my hand when the pastor asked, as he regularly did, how many of the girls were going to be nuns. I had read about Catherine of Siena in the Gold Medal lives of the saints supplied by the nuns. I explained to my friends that I was taking the confirmation name of Catherine after her, a laywoman who traveled a lot and influenced popes and queens. Another name, another identity. More than Catherine, however, it was Nancy Drew, whose first name and naturally curly hair I shared, who inspired me with her clever enterprise, as did *Little Women*'s Jo, a tomboy like me. And believe it or not, Little Orphan Annie commanding her troops in World War II, as our school collected scrap metal for the war effort, saved tinfoil in huge balls, and planted our little victory gardens.

My friends—Bev, Jan, Roz—and I thought we led

such wonderfully adventurous lives that Jan and I vowed to write an account of it and signed our pact with an "X" marked in our blood. Unlike today's children, who have to make play dates, be driven everywhere by their parents, and follow rigid schedules for soccer practice and gymnastics, we were "free-range chickens," roaming all over Black Rock and beyond on our bikes. We rowed, unaccompanied, out into Black Rock harbor in my father's big flat-bottomed boat. We made our way by two buses to the other end of Bridgeport to go horseback riding, and climbed, untaught, onto our horses, mine a large, heavy-footed creature named Comanche. In summer, having been awakened in the early morning by pebbles my friends threw at my window, I climbed down the roof outside my bedroom to the back porch—I could have used the door, of course—and we sneaked into the exclusive Black Rock Yacht Club to go skinny-dipping in its pool.

But all was not sunshine and play. Margaret Atwood captures both the camaraderie and—uniquely, to my knowledge—the cruelty of girls this age in *The Cat's Eye*. The four of us enlarged our circle to form a club called the Sevenerettes, whose chief purpose was to take turns telling each girl her faults. Not mentioned among them, however, was our unkindness to one another, and more brutally, "in thought, word, and deed," to those girls excluded from our membership. This is what we should have been saying in confession, instead of "I disobeyed my mother three times," or "I fought with my sister"—always three times.

And I had questions, doubts about the teaching of the church. I stood up in the seventh grade to ask, "How come God gets all the credit when I do something good, and I get all the blame when I do something bad?"—confronting the theological conundrum of grace and free will. I wrote, secretly, to the question-and-answer column in the diocesan newspaper to ask about Adam and Eve and evolution. The priest answered me with the equivalent of "Don't worry about such things, little girl."

And like all children, I had deeper secrets. When, in the sixth grade, Sister Josepha took me to the chart at the back of the room to show me the big dip in my marks, I did not tell her that I was worried sick, praying every night that my mother wouldn't go to hell. I didn't know this had anything to do with my marks. And not knowing anything about sex, I didn't understand what my mother meant when she said that she wasn't doing "anything wrong" in receiving frequent phone calls from the Irish tenor whose accompanist she was, often lunching with him, spending part of one Christmas Eve at his house. I thought she was "committing adultery." Maybe for the first time in her life she was in love, but she was not committing adultery. My father's reaction to the "affair" was to go out every night to the Algonquin Club and get drunk. Bobsey—my only sibling, five years older—and I never talked to each other about any of our family problems until some years later, and when we did, I trembled. So religion was my trap here, teaching me commandments I was too young to grasp, and prayer was my sole release. Books might have helped had the sort used in bibliotherapy for children existed. Reading stories about troubled marriages in other families, about coping with the possibility of my parents' divorce (my heart-chilling fear!) might, accompanied by appropriate guidance, have lessened my burden. But that was beyond the times and beyond the reach of all of us. And even had I known it, I didn't have enough experience then to agree or disagree with the first line of Tolstoy's *Anna Karenina:* "All happy families resemble one another. But each unhappy family is unhappy in its own way." I thought mine was the only unhappy family.

By the time I entered high school at Lauralton Hall, a Catholic girls' school in Milford, Connecticut, the religion game was all over. Now competition was for boyfriends, and the anonymous little slips of paper in the question box at our annual retreats were concerned with whether French kissing was a mortal or a venial sin. Confession, most terrifyingly of impure thoughts and feelings, was to be endured in order to be able to go to communion; it was noticed if you didn't, especially by your parents. And we ourselves noticed when one of our friends didn't "receive," assuming, little gossips that we were, that she and her boyfriend had crossed the line—the kissing and petting line; no one but notoriously fast girls went "all the way" in those days.

And since neither our parents nor teachers would tell us the facts of life—we waited in vain to get to the back of our junior-year religion textbook, where "purity" was (very abstractly) dealt with—I spent my adolescence looking for sexy books in the small Black Rock public library. I checked them out with a nonchalance feigned for the benefit of the ever-present Miss Hall, the librarian, and read them late into the night until my face was swollen, a towel stuffed under my door to conceal my bedroom light from my parents. *Studs Lonigan* was being passed around by the boys at Fairfield Beach and *A Tree Grows in Brooklyn* had been, scandalously, on the best-seller list. Because my sister had brought home Norman Mailer's *The Naked and the Dead* from college, I read that too. And it was there that I first came upon the "f word," though in its modified "fug-gin" form; until then, I had thought that the term "four-letter words" meant *hell, damn,* and *shit.*

When I think back to those times now, I am filled with astonishment and regret. We were so innocent, led such protected lives; my grandniece had already asked about "fuck" when she was nine. I am dumbfounded to know what a youngster should be given to read in our hyped, celebrity-crazed, highly sexualized culture. And I regret that no one directed my reading, bright as I was, to better books, to the classic novels, which for some reason were not part of my high school curriculum. My parents cer-tainly could not have done this for me. They didn't have the background, and anyway, they were beset by a difficult marriage and by the nagging financial difficulties we suf-fered as a result of my father's frequent depressions, dur-ing which little money came in from his business. Every time I pass the teenage girls on City Island Avenue, with their magenta lipstick and tight jeans, dancing around the boys, I regret that I can't tell them, as I would like to have been told, that there is a self within them, worthy of their own esteem, precious to God, and quite independent of the opinion of the little buggers whose attention they are so desperately trying to attract.

As it was, I sat in the car if I happened to be with my father when he made his daily visit to church. When I was a child, I had waited longer and more frequently for him outside the bar next to the butcher shop where we would go to get the meat for supper. But waiting outside church strikes me now as sadder. Maybe because this was an act of my own callow choosing, heedless not only of God but of my father and whatever it was of faith or need or both that sent him to church every day.

Thus it was as a rather brittle, superficially sophisticated young woman that I entered the College of New Rochelle, a Catholic women's college founded by the Ursuline nuns in New Rochelle, New York. The decision to go to college had been my own, as my sister's had been for her; my parents, though cooperative, had not insisted on it for either of us. At that time, there were very few coed Catholic colleges, and attending a secular college where you might lose your faith was more than discouraged by the nuns at Lauralton. So off to CNR I went. And there the world changed for me. I changed. Thinking that I was—wanting to be—like a glamorous character in a Scott Fitzgerald novel, I came to an about-face turn in the labyrinthine search for a true self.

Reflection

For me the act of reading is like the act of eating. That is how I experience it—a devouring of the words on the page, a taking into myself, the fulfillment of some elemental need. When I was a little girl I used to read the words on the cereal box at breakfast, my father's Veterans of Foreign Wars notices, anything. At one stage—fifth grade?—I pored over every word in every ad in the magazines that came into the house. I remember puzzling over the Kotex ads; I couldn't make out from the discreet wording what was wrong with the droopy young woman in the picture, or what this mysterious product was. I asked my sister and my mother repeatedly, and was excited to find a box of Kotex in the drugstore window. "There it is! There it is!" I said. "What is it? What is it?" But they answered that they didn't know either.

So what is it, this appetite for reading? I have often thought when watching nature programs on TV that the most basic act of animate nature is eating—not mating, which most animals do only when the female is in estrus. Everything living is eating something else in order to stay alive. That is why I read, I guess, to stay alive, to be as fully alive as I can be. In books, almost the whole world and everything in it are available to me to feed that life. The words we usually use to name that appetite—*interest, curiosity*—aren't good enough to describe the impulse, and *pleasure* doesn't adequately describe its satisfaction. It is the need to know and understand—myself, others, the world beyond me, God—to ask about what is real and true and good and of value, about how we should live our lives.

And so I read history and the little bit of science that I can grasp in order to learn about the world outside of myself. But since, especially in the realm of human personality and relationships, "facts are a very inferior form of fiction," as Virginia Woolf said, I read fiction. I read it not because I expect to find ready-made answers to my questions, but because I want to understand human life, both as it is and as it might be. And in good fiction I can observe the characters asking—or failing to ask, or wrongly answering—the questions that make us authentic human beings, true selves, the questions that are the very stuff of our lives, and the very stuff of literature, both tragic and comic. Here's what I mean.

According to Jesuit philosopher/theologian Bernard

Lonergan, it is our capacity to ask questions that go beyond what we already know that makes us self-transcending beings and puts us on the road to authenticity. *Capacity* is the key word here. We and our literary counterparts can, but don't always, follow the self-transcending path; sometimes just because we're not paying attention, we take a wrong turn, make mistakes. Out of blameless ignorance, or willfully, we don't ask the questions that would bring us to understand what is really the case. Or we don't reflect on what we think, asking whether it is really true apart from ourselves—our guesses, our pet theories, our wishes. We have questions about what we should do, how we should act. And we can make decisions that are right, based on objective value, on the truly good. But we make erroneous and bad ones too. Following the powerful impulses of passion, laziness, selfishness, weakness, prejudice, we choose what we want even when it is not good for us, and regardless of the good of others.

In all these ways, we and the characters we read about achieve, fail at, or refuse the self-transcendence implicit in our questioning. We zigzag between the authenticity that is achieved in self-transcendence and the inauthenticity of choosing or settling for less than we can be. Isn't it just these zigzagging lines that we follow in the endless variations of plot and character in all worthwhile fiction, as we observe the questions the protagonists ask (or don't ask), the answers they arrive at, and the consequences of their choices? But our questioning—our questing—is unending, unrestricted. There is always more to know and understand, more that we can become. And so we keep on reading. And so each book, no matter how fine, impels us to yet another.

Further, according to Lonergan, this capacity for unrestricted questioning, including the question (the question itself, not the answer) of whether there is a God or not, "presuppose[s] the spark in our clod, our native orientation to the divine." Or as Augustine said more simply, we are *capax Dei*—have the capacity for God, for perfect truth, goodness, love. And thus he said more famously, "Thou hast made us for Thyself, O God, and our hearts are restless until they rest in Thee."

"Every time you open a book you engage in an act of self-transcendence," observed a friend on first hearing of my intention to explore a spirituality of reading. He was a great reader himself and caught my drift immediately, although he was an areligious man who had probably never heard of Lonergan. But the matter is not quite so straightforward. Some books diminish us, simplify to the point

of distortion, falsify the facts, tell only half the story of
who we are as human beings. We need to be intelligent,
discerning, responsible readers. You are what you eat, as
the folk saying goes. And you are, in some ways, what
you read.

"TAKE AND READ"

A Turning Point

AUGUSTINE HEARD a child's voice, mysteriously, in the garden, chanting, "Take and read, take and read." Weeping, caught in the chain of indecision between the pleasures of the flesh, well known to him, and the sweet, calm call of chastity embodied in the child's voice, he snatched up the book he had put down, and opened it. Silently reading the first verse his eyes fell upon, he saw himself, as he was and as he wished to be: "not in reveling and drunkenness, not in debauchery and licentiousness, not in quarreling and jealousy. Instead, put on the Lord Jesus Christ; and make no provision for the flesh, to gratify its desires" (Romans 13:13ff). "I had no wish to read further," he tells us in his *Confessions*, "nor did I need to. For instantly, even with the end of this sentence, as if by a light of confidence infused into my heart, all the darkness of doubt vanished."

So St. Augustine describes his conversion, not only as a turning to a new way of life, but as the birth of a new self. It is intriguing to me that he, who marveled at Ambrose reading silently, was born anew in an act of silent reading. And that he, who had been a teacher of rhetoric, the spoken word, became the author of one of the earliest—and greatest—pieces of introspective Western literature, a work that is a marker on the journey of the human race to greater interiority. For writing and reading not only contribute to but also record that journey, one that we can follow from the flat characters of Homer's heroes, whose thoughts and motives are credited to gods and goddesses external to the self, all the way to the complex interiority of the modern novel. Thus the man whose conversion began with reading, and who later said that he found God *interior intimo meo*, more inner than his inmost self, serves as an emblem for a spirituality of reading, the journey into the self that we are taking in this literary labyrinth.

For most of us, however, conversion does not happen so dramatically, nor is it so dramatically occasioned by reading. We bumble along in life and in books, especially

in our youth, trying on one identity and another, often using fiction as "a relatively cost-free offer of trial runs" for
who we might be, who we might become, as Wayne Booth
puts it in *The Company We Keep: An Ethics of Fiction*.

Captivated by the heady glamour in the novels of
F. Scott Fitzgerald, I made a run for the real thing in my
first year at college. After the New York City St. Patrick's
Day parade, a friend of mine and I—she was the rebel in
our crowd—spent the night at a midtown hotel with boyfriends from her hometown, risking no less than expulsion
from CNR. Noise, a smoke-filled room, music, drinking,
all very Fitzgeraldesque. Then the house detective burst
into the room, shouting accusations. Terror. The rebel
countered that she would accuse him of rape. I lied to him
about my name and school and rode the train to Bridgeport the next morning with dry heaves all the way. My sister took one look at me, sent me to bed, and brought me
tea and cinnamon toast. Not quite cost-free, but valuable,
and a significant turning point in my life. I began to shed
that falsely sophisticated persona I had acquired. My
friend transferred to a secular college at the end of the
year. I did not give up reading Fitzgerald.

It is tempting to make fun of my sophomoric self beginning to ask the Big Questions in late-night conversations with my roommate, and reading Thomas Wolfe's

Look Homeward, Angel and *You Can't Go Home Again* in search of answers. At least that is what I think I was doing, and I found something in those books then—some sense of the largeness and drama of life that matched my own desires. I loved Turgenev's *Fathers and Sons* and Santayana's *The Last Puritan,* too, for the quality of calm wholeness I found in them.

And I was introduced to modern Catholic French literature: the novels, poetry, drama, and essays of Georges Bernanos, François Mauriac, Paul Claudel, Charles Péguy, Léon Bloy, Jacques and Raissa Maritain. They were leaders of the Catholic literary/intellectual renascence that took place in France in the first half of the twentieth century, highly regarded by the intelligentsia of their own country and beyond (Claudel was elected to the French Academy in 1946; Mauriac was awarded the Nobel Prize for literature in 1952). Here was a body of Catholic literature such as I had never encountered before. It was searching, profound, intelligent; it grappled with the dilemmas of the human condition itself, and though informed by Catholic belief, did not look to an easy piety for answers.

Thus, in my reading and in my studies, I was beginning to discover that learning has to do not only with facts but also with ideas, and that there is such a thing as an intellectual life—specifically, a Catholic intellectual life. I remember the great excitement with which I learned about the foreshadowings of Christ in the "Old Testament" (biblical typology was the thing then), and with which I explained the mystery of the Trinity to my mother as she was cooking dinner. When I sought a response from her as to what she made of it all, she said she just believed what she was told; I don't think she had ever given the Trinity a moment's thought.

Unlike her, I was still questioning. I had gone to the library card catalogue in my sophomore year to check out the listing "Freud" and had found only one entry, under the title *Seven Modern Devils*. Mother Judith (Ursulines were called "Mother" at the time), my philosophy teacher, explained to me that it was deemed wise that we be thoroughly grounded in the truth before we dealt with people like Freud. I was half convinced. And in a required junior-year history course, Christian Tradition and Culture, which was organized around the notion of the incarnation of Jesus Christ as the central event of history, I was skeptical. More important than World War II? I couldn't see it.

These were real conflicts in me, each of a different nature. I had too few arrows in my intellectual quiver to make a case for or against Kant, Freud, Marx, or whoever else was thought at the time to be an enemy of the truth. As for Jesus, I had no realization of the enormous influence of this man from Nazareth on the course of history. In both cases, even though I was a practicing Catholic who by junior year was thinking of becoming a nun, I gave to the tenets of Catholicism what Cardinal Newman called notional rather than real assent. I was of two minds, lacking the kind of faith that informs one's world view, one's life, including one's intellectual life.

At the same time, I was discovering, to my articulated amazement, that the spiritual life is just that—a life, something living and growing within us—and not merely a matter of keeping rules and regulations and fulfilling religious obligations. As I came to understand later, spirituality is meant to be the living breath, the soul, enlivening the creed, moral code, and cult—worship—that constitute any religion (if only our religious institutions and traditions would offer them to us as such). And this same vital force calls us to move us beyond personal piety and "giving good example" to address issues in the larger world.

I caught a glimpse of this dimension of spirituality through learning to read scripture in a new way. In freshman year, I had been tapped to become a member of a secret movement known as Young Christian Students, YCS. Following the model of the French lay apostolate called the Jocists, we met in cells to read and reflect on the Gospel together and, in its light, to "observe, judge, and act," not on matters of social justice as the Jocists did, but on tamer concerns such as life in the dorms and apathy on campus. Later, a few of us from New Rochelle formed a cell with guys from CCNY and Manhattan College, and things got more interesting. We held our meetings, sometimes in smoky bars and in cold basement rooms at City College, with no less a goal than infiltrating higher education and "restoring all things in Christ." This was a far cry from the glitter of a Fitzgerald novel, but it had its own kind of gritty romanticism and heady excitement, as, in our youthful idealism, we thought that we could change the world.

Still, there were plenty of rules and regulations at New Rochelle, and demerits applied if you broke them. A dress code required stockings at all times, hats or beanies if you went downtown, dressing up for a served dinner. Slacks were allowed only in the dorm. Permission had to be gotten for weekend dates, or to go into New York City, even to go home. Lights out was at ten, after obligatory night prayers led by the resident nun on every corridor. Attendance was taken at assemblies, lectures, religious exercises, and Sunday mass—a high-church liturgy with clouds of incense, gorgeous flowers and vestments, and Gregorian chant beautifully sung by a student choir—all of us garbed in academic caps and gowns.

Once, during freshman year, I decided to cut a Lenten talk, and was immediately summoned to the dean's office. I told Mother St. John that I would willingly take the three demerits assigned for the offense, figuring I had enough to spare before incurring the penalty of confinement to campus for a weekend. She, patiently, tried to tell me that my values were wrong, that I was missing the point. Maybe I was. As were most of us in our three-day annual Jesuit retreat, during which strict silence was to be observed and my friends and I joked about the old priest who told us over and over again "not to become someone's soiled plaything, tootsy-wootsy." But maybe the distinction that Mother was trying to get me to see between the substance of my act and the demerits would have been clearer had there been more substance to the talks.

The nuns, intelligent, well educated, most of them young, took a keen personal interest in us. Single-heartedly dedicated to the education of women, by which was meant the formation of good Catholic wives and mothers, they were the professors in many of our classes, omnipresent in the dorm, the cafeteria, at extracurricular activities. I began attending the early-morning meditations given before mass by Mother Thérèse, a powerful woman. We were directed to choose a "spiritual mother" from among the nuns; I chose Mother Denis, and, trembling again, I confided my family troubles to her.

So this was the fifties. The center still held, in society and more so in American Catholicism, still in many ways an immigrant church. The Enlightenment had not yet overtaken it, or at least had not made its way into institutions like ours. From our standpoint, if faith and reason were at odds, faith always won. We could be triumphalistic, as we were, because we had the truth in the "deposit of faith," on which we sat secure in our citadel, unexposed to the critical intellectual issues of the wider world.

But all of this—the ideas I encountered in my reading and my studies, the beauty of the liturgy, the example of dedicated lives, my own fledgling efforts at prayer— offered a compelling vision to the young person I was. I thought I had a vocation, and decided to become a nun, choosing more a way of life, I think now, than a relationship with God.

Like any major decision in life, it was complicated and with far-reaching consequences, more than I knew at twenty-one, as were the decisions of my classmates who were becoming engaged. Hardly considering the vows of poverty and obedience, I gave a lot of agonized thought to giving up love, marriage, and a family. I had dated guys at home and from YCS. And in my senior year, fellow YCS member Bill Kelly fell in love with me. I was not in love with him, but Graham Greene's *The Heart of the Matter* caught for me the timbre of the conflict between flesh and spirit that I was engaged in. I might find Greene a bit over-dramatic now, or more accurately, I might (as I think people reading Greene or Evelyn Waugh's *Brideshead Revisited* today might) have lost a sense for the sharp edge of the conflict. But it was real, and wrenching then. And since the Ursulines were semi-cloistered at the time, going out only for purposes of health and education, my decision meant that though my family could visit me at the convent once a month, I could not go home. And until after Vatican II, I did not, even for my father's funeral in 1958.

In the summer before I graduated from college and entered the convent, my friends at Fairfield Beach and I were reading Sigrid Undset's *Kristin Lavransdatter*, addressing each other in "thees" and "thous," and referring to the pregnant women among us as "great with child." For all the fun, we were—I was—overwhelmed by the trilogy. (An English translation of volume 1, *The Wreath*, in contemporary speech appeared in 1997.) Nobel Prize winner Undset was a convert to Catholicism, yet her work was not thought of as "Catholic," as in some ways Greene's and Waugh's were. But in its descriptions of passionate love and the dissolution of it under the weight of the mystery of another human personality; of the dreadful realities of war, the death of children, misunderstanding, betrayal; of endurance and faith, it is catholic, its symbolism universal. I count it among the most powerful books I have read, and wish my still-young self had "read" my parents' story as sympathetically and as generously as I read Kristin and Erland's. It took falling in love myself for me to understand my mother, and not only to forgive her for the unhappiness she had brought to our family, but to admire her fidelity to her marriage vows. And it took years before it occurred to me that my father could have responded to the situation in ways more helpful to himself and to his children than drinking.

On July 15, 1953, I said goodbye to my parents and sister. I don't remember anything else about the farewells except that my father, in a depression, kissed me goodbye at the top of the stairs and left for his office at the usual time, as if it were any other day in our lives. I went by train to Beacon, New York, smoked, I thought, my last cigarette, and walked through the gates of Hiddenbrooke, the Ursu-

line novitiate. It felt like a great and worthy venture—
costly, but safe. I imagined that I would become a nun,
come back to teach at the college, and inspire young
women as I had been inspired. "Heaven-Haven: A Nun
Takes the Veil," by Gerard Manley Hopkins, expressed my
feelings and hopes exactly:

> I have desired to go
> Where springs not fail,
> To fields where flies no sharp and sided hail
> And a few lilies blow.
>
> And I have asked to be
> Where no storms come,
> Where the green swell is in the havens dumb,
> And out of the swing of the sea.

At the time, nobody divined the sea change that Vatican II would bring to the church in general and to religious
life in particular. I certainly did not. Nor did it occur to me
that I was giving up reading any but spiritual books. For
the next fifteen years, as it happened, I would not read one
novel, one mystery story, not one "secular" biography or
autobiography. In "renouncing the world," I was renouncing the world of books. And I didn't even know it.

Reflection

Granny Maraffi never threw away a piece of bread without kissing it first. I imagine that this act of hers was rooted in her reverence for the consecrated bread of the eucharist, in which, Catholics believe, he who called himself the "bread of life" (John 6:35) is made present. By extension, as it were, all bread became holy for her. It was not a sacrament, but it was "sacramental"—grace-bearing—like the water, oils, incense, candles, palms, ashes, blessed by the church for worship and devotion. Granny's act symbolizes the sacramental universe that Catholicism inhabits: all creation is "charged with the grandeur of God"; and by the incarnation of Jesus Christ, human life and the world in all its materiality are yet more hallowed.

Like bread for my grandmother, books seem to carry a sacred weight for many of us, perhaps, for "people of the Book," because of the Bible. Jewish congregants kiss or reverently touch the Torah carried in procession during holiday services, and in Jewish Kabbalistic tradition the very letters of the alphabet are deemed holy. The priest at mass kisses the Gospel book after reading from it, and at solemn liturgies swings an incense-burning censer around it. As novices, we were trained never to place anything on top of our Bibles. Less immediately related to the sacred, however, I think that we pay a certain reverence to books because they contain so much of human creativity, hope, effort—represent someone's personhood. And I suspect that I am not alone in never having thrown a book, no matter how bad, in the wastebasket—with or without a kiss.

This attitude toward books is changing, I'm afraid. Low-cost mass production seems to diminish our sense of the sacredness of things, of food, of books, even of the Bible. Half a dozen years ago, I had the privilege of being at a conference with practicing Muslims. The reverence with which they handled their beautifully ornamented and scripted Ku'ran made me guiltily aware of my own dog-eared, written-in paperback Bible placed casually on the floor beside my chair. As a Catholic, I am glad the days of chained Bibles are long gone and that we have easy access to the word of God. But perhaps I have become too famil-iar in my treatment of it; maybe I should kiss the Bible after reading it. Now, too, the thick leather-bound daily missals with gilt-edged onionskin pages, which some Catholics owned and used at mass, have given way to seasonal missalettes. Found in the pews of most parish churches, they are available to all. But they are paper-covered, printed on cheap gray stock—disposable. I am sure they are simply thrown away when outdated, or recycled, like newspapers and magazines.

Still, although I may have lost a sense of reverence for the sacred books themselves, the same sacramental principle that finds God in all things has impelled me to explore a spirituality of reading in different kinds of books, not just explicitly spiritual ones. Because in them, and especially in good novels, I find the astonishing richness of God's world—human, animate, inanimate—celebrated in all its *haeccitas,* its "thisness" (just the opposite of the mass-produced), as Duns Scotus named it.

Patrick O'Brian's twenty Aubrey/Maturin novels—I have read eight—set aboard British frigates in the Napoleonic wars, deliver thisness in abundance. When we board ship with the tall, blond, openhearted Captain Aubrey and Stephen Maturin, his ship's surgeon, a smaller, more complex man, a naturalist and a spy for the British to boot, we are invited to sample from the cargo a rich store of information of all sorts. I read the sailing lore with interest, if not with much comprehension, and follow the historically accurate battles as best I can—not always effortlessly, since the British ships captured from the French still carry their French "baptismal" names.

But it is the detail about life aboard ship that intrigues and delights me: how the sailors washed, braided, and oiled their hair every three months or so; what they ate in the different messes (the ship's numerous rats when provisions were low) along with their daily ration of grog; that the ships carried animals—goats and fowl—and some of Maturin's specimens, flora and fauna, large and small, about which we are instructed along the way. We find out that women were occasionally smuggled aboard for carnal purposes, and that boys as young as eight, who served as the surgeons' assistants, were sometimes killed in battle, wrapped in canvas, and thrown overboard "like a little pudding." How church was rigged on Sunday; when the good-natured Aubrey judged it necessary to discipline a sailor by flogging; the ways in which politics, class, and economics figured in the picture (the hands got a share of the prize on capturing an enemy ship). We learn that Aubrey and Maturin played violin and cello duets in the captain's spacious cabin at night; that the crew danced, put on operettas; and that some of the officers wrote and declaimed their own poetry. And more—all of it, the thisness of it—bringing me to wonder at the variety and abundance in human life as much as I wonder at them in the world of nature.

I suppose I could have gotten the facts I gleaned from reading O'Brian in a nautical encyclopedia of some sort, but I never would have made the effort, or even known that I could be interested. Here the knowledge comes easily, buoyed up by plots of action, intrigue, and romance, an especially fascinating one carried on from book to book between Maturin—and at one point, Aubrey—and the capricious Diana Villiers. The characterization is complex enough to be interesting, the language carefully crafted, with charmingly archaic dialogue that I take to be authentic to the period (the characters sometimes refer to God as "the Dear").

A decade ago in Boston I visited the USS *Constitution*, Old Ironsides, which figures as an enemy ship in one of the novels, and was amazed at how *small* it is. How could it have carried all that it did: four hundred fifty men, gunpowder and cannonballs, thousands of gallons of water, provisions, several galleys, a surgery, a carpentry? More amazing to me is how O'Brian in a prodigious—one of Aubrey's words—feat of knowledge and imagination has (re)created a world between the covers of a dozen-plus books. So his work is a cause for celebration, not only of the stuff of life presented in its bounteous thisness, but of the Author of it all whose creativity O'Brian reflects and "incarnates" in his books: creation and incarnation in one. And then, in my reading of the book, words made flesh—real—yet again in my mind's eye. It looks like a book, but it is a world. A marvelous alchemy. Or better, a transubstantiation, a sacrament.

"NOT BY BREAD ALONE"

Spiritual Reading in a Literary Desert

THIS IS NOT *The Nun's Story*. Nor is this book meant to be primarily about spiritual reading as such. But spiritual reading is reading, and a significant practice in the spirituality of various religious traditions. As young nuns, except for purposes of study, we were not permitted to read anything else. The matter was not open for discussion; "worldly" books and magazines were simply not available. So what did I learn from the concentration and deprivations of that period?

In pre–Vatican II Ursuline life, approximately five hours a day were devoted to spiritual exercises: mass, meditation, the chanting of Office in choir, the saying of the rosary, an examination of conscience, all of which, except the last two, entailed reading in one way or another; one half hour was given specifically to private spiritual reading. With the exception of feast days, when we were permitted to talk to one another at meals, we were read to during lunch and dinner, each of us taking her turn a week at a time at the reader's desk. At breakfast, and for the rest of the day, not counting the recreation periods after lunch and dinner, we observed a rule of silence.

We did not think it odd to begin our meals listening to a brief account from the Roman Martyrology commemorating the martyrs and saints who had died on that day. We spooned our soup to tales of eyes being plucked out, limbs torn asunder, and flesh roasted, and our healthy young appetites were not diminished a bit. The Martyrology was followed by the reading of the lives of the saints or books about spirituality, all selected by the superior; most of these books, I must confess, I don't remember. What I do remember, however, are the instances when the reader's mistake sent us into such convulsions of uncontrollable laughter—the suppressed, snorting kind, as occurs in church—that the superior was compelled to ring her little bell, stop the reading, and permit us to talk to one another. My very favorite mistake, recalled from a dozen years later, and made simply by reading a feminine for a masculine pronoun—"He stroked his beard," said the text—had our sixteenth-century founder St. Angela Merici performing this action on Pope Clement VII. Reverend Mother had to ring the bell on that one.

We Ursulines, like most religious communities today—although I just heard of one that listens to taped books—no longer follow the practice of reading in the refectory. But along with what has been gained in easy congress with one another, perhaps we have lost the benefits that this kind of shared reading brought us. I believe now that greatest of them wasn't the edification we were supposed to derive from what we heard, it was the sense of community that it engendered. Think of it: a group of people, virtually every day for decades, hearing the same books read. There were the good books to be analyzed and discussed later, providing an ever-ready topic of conversation, a shared point of reference; the unpopular books that united us in common suffering to the very last page, and about which we had our private opinons, communicated to one another by making a face or rolling our eyes (one didn't openly criticize Reverend Mother's selections); the occasions of hilarity remembered for years the way family jokes are. And it was compulsory: if you wanted to eat, you could hardly avoid listening. I can't think of any programs of shared reading, even with all the varieties of book clubs available now, that can compare with the rigor of this regime, or that contribute to community building as much as this did.

For our private spiritual reading, postulants—newcomers—were given, as required reading, two books: Thomas à Kempis's *Imitation of Christ* and *The Practice of Perfection and of Christian Virtues*, by Alphonsus Rodriguez, S.J. *The Imitation of Christ*, a little book written in Latin in 1441, and translated into English in 1470, is considered something of a spiritual classic, and epitomizes in what is perhaps its most famous sentence the flight from the world that characterized monastic piety before Vatican II: "I never leave my cell but what I return less a man." A contemporary edition of *The Imitation* has this quote from William Thackeray about the book: "The scheme of that book carried out would make the world the most wretched, useless, dreary, doting place of sojourn . . . a set of selfish beings crawling about avoiding one another, and howling a perpetual *miserere*," no doubt an attempt on the part of the editor to disarm the reader before pointing to the merits of the book. I wouldn't have put my feelings about *The Imitation* as strongly as Thackeray did, but I don't know to this day what it was supposed to offer a young, educated American woman.

Rodriguez's work, three large volumes written in the
sixteenth century as a manual for Jesuit novices in Spain,
contains treatises on the vows of poverty, chastity, and
obedience, and the virtues of the Christian life. The virtue
of "detachment," for example, is dealt with under the title
"Of Other Evils and Losses Caused by Affection for Kindred, and How Christ Our Redeemer Taught Us to Keep
Out of Their Way." The treatises were followed by exem-
plary tales: "What Has Been Said Is Confirmed by Some
Examples"—like the one about the monk who for months
obediently watered a dry stick, which, of course, burst into
bloom at his death. The books were strange, alien to our
experience, but so was everything else in this new life of
ours: our long black habits; going to bed in the daylight;
kissing the floor as an act of penance; answering to religious names chosen to signal death to the old self and the
new identities we were assuming in the "second baptism"
of our vows (I took the name Mary Augusta after the
great saint and my father, William Augustine). When I
had read *The Imitation* fourteen times and Rodriguez
twice, I was given permission by Reverend Mother to read
something else.

Since we were not allowed as novices to read the classics, especially the mystics—Teresa of Ávila, John of the

Cross, the fourteenth-century English mystical writers—
lest we be drawn into illusory forms of prayer, I selected
from the novitiate library one of several lives of Christ
popular at the time. They were innocent of the historical-
critical method of contemporary biblical study that exam-
ines the literary genres of the Gospels and the times and
contexts in which they were composed. With a strong bent
toward apologetics, they stressed the divinity of Jesus: "All
His teaching, all His conduct, all His miracles tend to inculcate this truth in the mind of His hearers," as Abbot
Marmion, O.S.B., said in *Christ in His Mysteries*. The Jesus
they portrayed was a flat, undeveloped human character
whose every thought, word, and deed was presented to
teach us a lesson. How far from the springs of genuine human action, from a Jesus who acted out of compassion for
the woman who suffered for twelve years with a hemor-
rhage, or for the widow whose son had died. How unap-
pealing and boring, I thought—this Jesus, this book, and
not a few others.

Happily, however, I finally found two books in the library that nourished me and saw me through the rest of
the two-and-a-half-year novitiate; I read them over and
over. *The Lord*, by Romano Guardini, an Italian who grew
up in Germany and is best known as a leader in the Roman
Catholic liturgical renewal of the 1950s, is not so much a

life of Christ as reflections upon the person of Christ. It is true that the book presents a "Christology from above," as the title indicates. That is, like Marmion, Guardini premised belief in the divinity of Christ, the eternal Word. But he gave me as well a Jesus who was complex enough to be credibly human; he plumbed the depths of the humanity of the Word made flesh, whose fears, questions, pain, joys were like our own. And in *The Life and Letters of Janet Erskine Stuart*, an English Religious of the Sacred Heart (1857–1914), by Maud Monahan, a member of the same community, I found an educated, sensitive, witty woman, a modern woman, really, whose sane and generous under-standing of human nature reflected a large and compas-sionate God. Stuart's was the first serious biography I had ever read, and it was certainly the first that presented the life of someone saintly as anything less than impossibly heroic.

Over the years, I have read a lot of biography and au-tobiography, and though no one would think of canoniz-ing Meriwether Lewis, Eleanor and Franklin Roosevelt, Virginia Woolf, or Katharine Graham, I regard these books as spiritual reading. All of them—like many others—refract the mystery of a human life, with its challenges, accomplishments, failures, and suffering, and a human personality in its ineluctable givenness. And each answers in its unique way the questions I am always asking when I am reading: What is it all about? I mean life, its meaning and purpose. And what do other people make of it, not only in their thinking but in their doing? What do they make of themselves, in both senses of the phrase? What can they change about themselves, and what not; what is their destiny, fate, vocation? Whom do they love and why? Do they love foolishly or wisely? These are, to my way of thinking, religious questions, matters of "ultimate concern," in the words of Protestant theologian Paul Tillich. Whether they are referred to God or not, these questions and the answers we give them are, finally, ultimate for each of us; they frame and guide the one life each of us has to live.

And they are the questions the gifted biographer answers for us. She, like God in a way, while affirming the good in her subject, is not ignorant of and does not gloss over faults and weaknesses, even great ones, but understands and accepts them, and helps the reader to do the same. Hermione Lee, author of the monumental biography of Virginia Woolf, acknowledges the writer's snobbery, her qualified anti-Semitism, the occasional meanness of her wit. Nonetheless, I left the book with an enormous admiration for the woman who, afflicted with crippling illness of body and mind, struggled faithfully, every day that she was minimally able, to get out of bed and do what she was called to do: write. In *No Ordinary Time*, Doris Kearns Goodwin, with remarkably balanced judgment, made me see how, given their personalities, Eleanor and Franklin Roosevelt simply could not have sustained an intimate relationship—neither was to blame and both were—but they achieved what they could together for a greater public good and at great personal cost.

I wrote to Katharine Graham, who assumed the office of president of *The Washington Post* after the suicide of her husband, Phil, to express my admiration for her and her memoir, *Personal History*. The book appeared in her eightieth year, and I thought the courage, fairness, and honesty she manifested in it and in her life extraordinary. I added that, not meaning to condemn, I, a Roman Catholic nun, was amazed at all that she suffered and achieved, without any mention of religious faith to sustain her. I got a brief but gracious response from Ms. Graham, thanking me. Then she wrote: "You mentioned the lack of any acknowledgment of religious faith in the book. I suppose it's because I grew up in a non-religious household. Religion just wasn't discussed or practiced. I was a product of that environment and, I guess, that comes through in the book. But

I was very pleased to hear . . ." The "But" unsettled me a bit; I had really meant what I said about not condemning. As I wrote in a brief review of the book for an in-house Ursuline publication: "So no religion, but an abundance, a surplus, of spirit."

I have been reflecting on why Stephen Ambrose's *Undaunted Courage,* a biography of Meriwether Lewis and an account of Lewis and Clarke's journey in search of the Northwest Passage, impressed me and others so much. Ambrose is a marvelous writer, his prose transparent of the realities he is describing—the physical hardship, the danger from nature and from the hostile Native American tribes, the element of unknownness in the undertaking, the political stakes, the array of different skills the explorers required to survive, all the while noting hitherto unrecorded facts about flora, fauna, topography. To have a life of such courage and accomplishment end in death from gunshot wounds that Ambrose deems self-inflicted, a suicide, brings us, the biographer and the reader, right up against imponderable mystery.

It is the rare life of a saint that achieves the kind of honesty and complexity I have found in these books. Quite purposely, Ida Friederike Goerres, one of Guardini's circle in the post–World War II German Catholic renascence, proposed to write such a book in *The Hidden Face,* her

1959 biography of Thérèse of Lisieux, the Little Flower. *The Story of a Soul*, Thérèse's autobiography, had been "touched up" by her blood sisters who were also members of the saint's religious community, as had the portraits of her painted by one of the sisters. With the best of intentions, they made both the portrait and the autobiography reflect an ideal saint—an ideal, nineteenth-century, French petit bourgeois saint—simple, perfect, sweet, almost saccharine. "She has been hidden from our sight by so many veils: the cheaply gilded veil of insipid bad taste; the opaque, rigid folds of an outmoded ideal of sainthood; the deceptive curtains of stylization," says Goerres.

And so in *The Hidden Face* the biographer carefully strips all these away. She uncovers the enormous cost of sanctity in the so-called "little way" of this young woman: the relentless but graceful fidelity to humdrum daily duty; her selfless service of and patience with her sisters, not all kind, not all mentally sound; her unflinching honesty; the complicated relationship she had with her attractive, erratic, self-indulgent superior; her humble perception of herself, coupled with the conviction of God's great love for her; and a faith tried by fire, especially during her excruciating and prolonged death at age twenty-four from tuberculosis, when she lived in utter darkness of spirit, clinging to faith only by a naked act of will.

But then even Goerres, who has revealed so much of a real human personality to us, using all available evidence, finally comes up against "the radiant gaze of Thérèse's own resolute silences which no human effort can entirely lift away." She bows before the mystery, the limitation, that even the gifted biographer must accept, that Ambrose had to accept. Only the novelist, the omniscient author, can read the deepest silences in another human being, which is one reason among others that I count some novels as spiritual reading.

As for most lives of the saints, until they offer enough insight into real human struggle to match the messy condition of my own interiority, I'll stick with secular biographies of worthy subjects by insightful, unprejudiced biographers who write well. Books like these afford us the deep pleasure of a kind of literary intimacy with their subjects. And as we come to know, understand, and accept these persons both in their "abundance of spirit" and their frailty, our own spirits are enriched. To put it in religious language, and to speak for myself, the books that I value have edified me, in the root meaning of the word; they have built me up and enlarged me. I am a wiser, more tolerant woman for having read them, less hard on others and even on myself.

I'm not going to name here all that has served me well as spiritual reading over the years; I have included a short selected bibliography at the end of this book. You might also consult Eugene H. Peterson's *Take & Read: Spiritual Reading: An Annotated List.* Urging readers to compile their own lists, the author charmingly advances his selections, taken from a variety of genres in Western literature. He includes some of my choices and omits others that I consider important, especially the books that are pursuing the conversation that the West is having and must have with the great world Eastern religions. I think of the many articles by Beatrice Bruteau and particularly of her book *What We Can Learn from the East* and of Diana Eck's *Encountering God.* Both women, though in different ways—Eck, with a good bit of her life story, Bruteau in reflection on her own spiritual experience—grapple personally with the issues of belief and practice that the Eastern religions raise for Christians, and show us as well how our own faith can be enriched by exposure to these ancient traditions.

Bruteau's articles and books have been especially helpful to me in my own labyrinthine search for self. In them, she illumines, among other things, the distinction between our descriptive selves—the real but limited roles we play in life: nun, editor, sister, friend, and in which so much of our ego is invested—and our true self, the natural self, as she calls it, or, borrowing a Zen koan, "the face we had before our parents were born." "By practicing the *via negativa* of denying that natural self's *identification* [italics mine] with these limited selves we come to the metaphysical/mystical meaning of self-denial." Now, there's an insight worth reading for, and a practice of self-denial a tad more difficult than going without salt on your eggs, as I faithfully did as a novice.

I had read Thérèse's *Story of a Soul* in the novitiate—it has all the faults that Goerres mentions above—and under the influence of my novice mistress, I thought I had some devotion to the saint and her "little way." But I was caught, egotistically, more by the goal of sanctity than by the little way to it. Having read Thomas Merton's *The Seven Storey Mountain* and *The Sign of Jonas,* the journal of the young monk's early years in the monastery, I pictured myself a female Merton, walking on the wooded paths in Beacon, lost in contemplation of God. Just like him when he wrote the journal, I was still in the honeymoon stage of my religious life, "first fervor," we call it. Actually, it was my own imagined holy self—walking on the wooded paths, lost in contemplation—that I was contemplating, not God. And I think now that one of the reasons I don't appreciate Merton—so many people whose judgment I respect do—is that I find too much of myself in him. It is not insignificant that one thing I remember from the biography of him by Michael Mott is that the psychiatrist whom Merton saw, without much success, told the monk, that yes, Merton wanted to be a hermit, but in the middle of Times Square with a red neon sign blinking "HERMIT."

By the time *The Hidden Face* came along to correct my ideas about genuine sanctity, I was teaching Latin and religion at The Ursuline School for girls in New Rochelle. During those years, from 1960 to 1965, I read and reread the book with great appreciation. I read it again on retreat several summers ago; it has borne, for me, the test of time. It is lucid, wise, beautifully written and translated, full of insight. A fine, fine book.

But back then, still far from *practicing* any "little way," I was chafing under the yoke of thwarted ambition. Why was I not being sent on for further study, as had been recommended by the great Latinist Martin R. P. McGuire, my mentor at Catholic University? Why wasn't I sent to the college to teach? Why was I put in charge of maintenance in the school building instead of an influential extracurricular activity like the sodality? Because, I was told privately by a member of the community government, Reverend Mother thought me "dangerous." Vatican II was under way, its fresh air just beginning to blow against the tightly sealed windows of the convent. I was right there with my nose pressed to the window frame and, influenced by Cardinal Suenens's groundbreaking *The Nun in the Modern World,* I and some others were convinced that our life had to change. That was dangerous enough. Still a redhead under my veil, I was impolitic, to say the least, in the ways I pursued the agenda of change. I was a disturber of the peace, and continued to be for many years.

In the summer of 1966, having been assigned to teach classics at the College of New Rochelle the year before, I was sent to the University of Michigan for a course in the Latin elegiac poets. During the compulsory physical examination, I was diagnosed with tuberculosis. Back in New Rochelle, quarantined in a tower room in the convent, I was permitted visitors only if they wore masks. I began taking Doriden for the insomnia I suffered as a result of my inactivity, and was given huge doses of nausea-inducing medication for the TB. I could not even listen to music; it had too much "motion" in it.

But I could read and did. Still restricted to spiritual reading, I was fortunate to come upon Ida Goerres's fascinating journal *Broken Lights.* In it she proposes the lovely notion of "book providence"—that certain books come into our lives at certain times for some God-given purpose, as hers had come to me in my confinement. It was in that book that I learned that she was a member of Guardini's circle in Germany. So I wrote to thank her for *Broken Lights* and *The Hidden Face,* and to suggest that since she and Guardini were among the authors who had influenced me most profoundly, perhaps there is a "book kinship" as well as a book providence.

The TB marked a turning point in my life. I was not able to meet my classes in the fall, and realized that I did not want to spend the rest of my days teaching Latin (the decision to study it had not been mine but my superior's). Attracted as I was to the world of ideas inhabited by people like Guardini and Goerres, and hoping that theology would help me make sense of life, I asked permission to enter that field. After two semesters at Notre Dame, where I was very unhappy, I transferred to the Harvard Divinity School in January 1968, garbed by then in a modified habit, still long, still black, but less voluminous, and with a simplified, less confining headdress. There I began to sort out the relationship between theology and spirituality, what it was that had attracted me to books like Guardini's, and why some "inspirational" books leave me cold. And for the first time since I entered the convent, I went home in September of that year, to celebrate my mother's seventieth birthday.

Reflection

When I first mentioned the idea of a spirituality of reading to others, some immediately said, "Oh yes, *lectio divina*." An ancient method of reading the scriptures going back to before the fifth century, when it was systematized, it calls for the slow, attentive, repetitive reading of a short passage from the Bible—it is suggested that the reading be done out loud—followed by meditation and then by prayer. But *lectio* is as much or more a method of prayer as of reading, and in its structure and use of and appeal to the imagination, it is similar to the Ignatian/Jesuit method of prayer that I was taught in the novitiate.

Struggling to stay awake at 5:30 A.M., I was to read a passage from scripture, imagine the biblical scene with myself in it, attend carefully to the meaning of what was said and done, apply it to my life, and end with a colloquy, a prayer addressed to God, Jesus, Mary, or one of the saints, asking for the grace suggested by the exercise. Distractions were to be mightily resisted.

"Systemic distraction." This is the term that Sharon Daloz Parks uses to describe the state we live in. Like systemic racism, distraction is not simply a matter of individual disposition and choice, but exists in and is encouraged by the very structures of contemporary postmodern life. In such a culture, the stillness, silence, solitude, and focused attention that reading offers is to be prized; it may be the closest some of us get to a spirit of contemplation in the hurried, noisy, scattered lives that we lead. A good book can create a little hermitage for some people anywhere, even in an airport waiting room. I envy them, and am only just beginning to understand why I so rarely read while traveling, especially if I am traveling on business.

Once, when I was on a train from New York to Boston, the little boy across the aisle, about four, I guessed, kept asking his mother, "Are we here yet?" Every time the train stopped, he asked, "Are we here yet?" I think he was on to something. The strictly correct answer to his question at each stop, and all along the way, was yes. But like Gertrude Stein on Oakland, California—"there's no there there"—I cannot find a "here" anywhere when I'm traveling with the intent of getting "there." My full consciousness is not available to me; I cannot give myself to a book. Instead, I slip into a brown funk, a kind of melancholy stupor. I should probably work on this as a spiritual discipline—"living fully in the moment," "being present," recalling that all life is "a journey, a pilgrimage."

And anyway, the plane might crash or the train derail, so I may as well die happy, reading.

In 1992–93, I spent most of December and January at the Ursuline generalate in Rome, attending a program devoted to studying the life of our founder. I loved Italy— the charmed and charming natural beauty of Northern Italy, St. Angela's birthplace, the overwhelming aesthetic richness of Rome, the humane pace of life everywhere. To my surprise I felt more at home there ethnically and spiritually than I had during a trip to Ireland some years before. But I could not read anything more demanding than mystery stories. I was using up too much of my psychic energy learning how to make a phone call, pay my fare on the buses, identify the meat at dinner (was that rabbit?), and taking in all the unfamiliar sights, sounds, and customs, not to mention being enveloped in another language.

And the same was true when I first moved to City Island. It was, in a way, like being in a foreign country, where new patterns had to be established for everything— shopping and cooking for myself, where to put things, when to take out the garbage and to pay the rent. I went through a couple of Sue Grafton's alphabet mysteries at that time and found private investigator Kinsey Millhone the perfect companion for the transition; the books were well written and engaging but did not ask too much of me.

I do not pray well when I am traveling, either. Besides my not being "there"—or "here"—the impersonality of hotel and conference center rooms, no matter how much more beautifully furnished than my own little digs, seems to rob me of myself. I lose a sense of who I am. Even in the generalate in the holy city of Rome, my journal records, "I can't find a place to pray." The chapel, with its dark, all-too-lifelike murals depicting scenes from Ursuline history, didn't appeal to me. It was too cold to sit or walk in the monastery garden, despite honest-to-goodness grapefruit and clementines ripe for the picking. And I couldn't find a comfortable chair anywhere—not one in the whole high-ceilinged, marble-floored building.

I know now, but only just now, that in these strange circumstances I should have adapted my praying, as I adapted my reading, to something less demanding. That is, I should have used something familiar, repetitive, like the rosary. Recently, I learned that the rosary, the repetition of the Our Father, the Hail Mary, the Glory Be, the fifty beads prayed three times in the course of a week to embrace the joyful, sorrowful, and glorious mysteries, was first used by the illiterate as a substitute for the reading and recitation of the one hundred fifty psalms of the psalter. When I am feeling "illiterate"—tired, mentally fatigued—I say it, often in the evening, walking slowly the twenty-five paces from one end of my rooms to the other. I no longer rush through it as I did when it was just one of many spiritual exercises that I was obliged to perform every day. I allow myself to float imaginatively in and out of the mysteries (the annunciation, the carrying of the cross, the descent of the Holy Spirit) and to linger over the words of the prayers ("full of grace," "fruit of thy womb"), stopping now and then to brush away a cobweb, straighten a chair, or drop something in the wastebasket. And because I do not expect perfect attention of myself, it seems my mind is free and receptive not to great theological insight but to the appreciation of how real and human the mysteries and the people in them are.

The need that some of us have to change our prayer and reading to suit our circumstances points to at least two kinds of readers and prayers: pilgrims and monks. There are those, like Muslims unfurling their prayer rugs no matter where they are and orienting themselves toward Mecca, who can find "here" anywhere. And there are those who need a "monastery." I am a monk. For me, focused reading and praying seem to require the same conditions: a certain stability, a sense of myself, the ability to give my full attention to what I am doing, and a degree of physical comfort.

Like many people, I have a favorite place and posture for reading and praying. I read propped up on pillows, on my couch or bed. And though I begin and end every day with a brief prayer on my knees, for longer periods of meditation I sit in my comfortable rocker. The lotus position this is not, nor do I have a philosophy of breathing and posture to justify it. If it sounds indolent, I reassure myself with the knowledge that St. Ignatius of Loyola, the founder of the Jesuits, allows in the Spiritual Exercises for many postures for prayer: "now kneeling, now prostrate upon the ground, *now lying face upwards* [italics mine], now seated, now standing." And like Carolyn Heilbrun, who reports in *The Last Gift of Time: Life Beyond Sixty* that she finally was free enough to defy the convention that required women to wear high heels and skirts for certain occasions, and to dress for comfort and utility in flats and slacks, I am free now to do what works for me; my body in these postures is not distracting to me. I pray more and more easily when I don't surround the act with formal, demanding conditions.

The eccentric French philosopher Simone Weil maintained that the kind of attention given to study prepared one for prayer. Maybe it works the other way around as well: maybe the kind of disciplined attention and imagination that I practiced in prayer during my fifteen-year sojourn in a literary desert has made me a better reader—if regrettably of fewer books.

THE CIRCLE WIDENS

Theology as Spiritual Reading?

GOING TO HARVARD WAS, for me, like leaving a large church with vaulted ceilings, warm with the smell of incense and candle wax, the light from its stained-glass windows making for mystery in dark corners, and stepping into the clear white light of an austere New England Congregational church. As one is in Protestant churches, I was genuinely welcomed by all at the Divinity School, even though I was something of an oddity in my habit, one of the first nuns to study there, and the only one during my course of study. I learned, slowly, that the clear white light—the generous, liberal, intelligent rationalism that prevailed in the halls of the school—creates

an atmosphere in which certain matters, like papal infalli-
bility, indulgences, or purgatory, for instance, are not ar-
gued about but are simply not spoken of. To raise them
would have made me feel guilty, not of erroneous thinking
or errant faith, but of having committed a social gaffe. It
would have been embarrassing. Here I found a faith different from that which I had always known, and it challenged
and chastened my own. I was, in a word, being baptized,
and by immersion, into the Enlightenment.

Much of what I experienced at HDS was new to me.
Except for a few childhood playmates, I had not known
any Protestants, and I had no sense of what makes a Bap-
tist different from an Episcopalian, or a Lutheran, or a
Presbyterian. I had never heard of Schliermacher, but I
knew the name Niebuhr, and so signed up for a course on
"Kant, Coleridge, and Schliermacher" with Richard R.
Niebuhr, son of H. Richard and nephew of Reinhold, two
great, though very different, twentieth-century Protestant
theologians. I wrote my first term paper for Niebuhr on
music and religion in Schliermacher and got an A for it.
When I was lacking in confidence, as I often was in this
high-powered atmosphere, I actually used to get up in the
middle of the night and look at that A as a way of reassur-
ing myself. And I became one of Niebuhr's disciples, tak-

ing a course from him each of the four semesters I was at Harvard. Naturally, what I was reading in these and other courses affected my thinking, and thus my spirituality. How could it not?

Under the rubric of religious experience, I read many of the theologians being studied in Protestant theology at the time: about despair and faith in Søren Kierkegaard's *Sickness unto Death* and *Fear and Trembling* and about the imagination in Coleridge. In *The Courage to Be*, Paul Tillich deals with the anxiety that we in our finitude experience in the face of nonbeing, death, meaninglessness, and guilt; to ask how courage is possible is, according to Tillich, to ask about God, the ground of being. I read Gabriel Marcel's *Homo Viator*, an exploration of what we are doing when we engage in an act of hope, and Jürgen Moltmann's *Theology of Hope*, an application of hope to the realm of the political. In Rudolph Otto, I learned of "the idea of the holy" as the *mysterium tremendum et fascinans*, the mystery that both terrifies us (causes us to tremble) and fascinates us, and in Mircea Eliade of the experiences of sacred time and place in earlier cultures. H. Richard Niebuhr's *The Meaning of Revelation* brought me to a nuanced understanding of how revelation can take place in human communities. I read Kant, too, and was able to understand what I was reading only as long as I kept my eyes glued to the page, like an evergreen branch that burns only as long as it is held to the flame.

Unlike the theology I had previously been exposed to, concerned with correct understanding of doctrine and morality as enshrined in scripture and the Catholic tradition, much of what I was reading for my courses began with the grounding of religious experience in human nature itself. This was new to me; it offered an approach to the study of God that I hadn't explored before. And it provided a foundation for understanding the relationship between theology and spirituality that I—and many others—came to a few years later when I was introduced to *The Transformation of Man* (1967), by Rosemary Haughton, a British convert to Catholicism, the mother of ten children, whose only degrees are honorary.

In this book, after giving us thick descriptions of human experience—a children's quarrel, a love affair, a man discovering his true self in midlife, the prophet Jeremiah, a family deciding to move, a Separatist community and that of St. Benedict—Rosemary, who later became a friend of mine, provided a theological analysis of what was going on in each situation—in terms, that is, of grace, faith, salvation, formation, transformation, and the like. She used this method, she said:

to create at least a small degree of actual involve-
ment in the situations described, so that the experiences referred to would be experienced. Then the
words used to describe the nature of these events
might possibly have the resonance of experimental
knowledge. You could call this experimental [I
would call it experiential] theology, but whatever
name it is given the idea arose from a conviction
that much theological discussion is wasted, not
because the words used have no possible meaning
but because the people who use them don't mean
anything by them. They don't know what the
words mean, even though they have almost certainly had precisely those experiences to which the
words refer.

To appreciate the originality of Rosemary's contribu-
tion in this book, we must remember back to those days
before Vatican II when Roman Catholic dogma was mostly
perceived as a set of propositions to which one gave intellectual assent—for example, one believed in the resurrection and had proofs about it lined up for use against
unbelievers (all of them drawn from scripture and the
teaching of the church, by the way, and therefore circular).
That an experience of the risen Lord might be available to

believers, or that the resurrection had any implication for one's life, personally or communally, was not given much attention. Rosemary's message was embodied in her medium—the novelistic accounts of everyday life and experience. No academic or ecclesiastical theologian in 1967 could or would have adopted this method, and not only because so many more of them in those days were male clerics. And although I have always remembered that phrase about not knowing "what the words mean" to refer to ordinary folk, I now think it could as well refer to those professional theologians, past and present, who forget—not all do— that theology is supposed to have some relationship to the lives of believers and to the life of the believing community as a whole.

No less rigorous a theologian than Bernard Lonergan himself saw the need for and appreciated the work of people like Rosemary. Fast forward to June 1977; I was again back in Massachusetts. We were in my very small living room on Orchard Street in Somerville, having dinner on the drop-leaf table pulled out for the occasion. My guests were Rosemary, Lonergan, and Bill Shea, a friend of mine and a disciple of Lonergan's. Bill knew how much Lonergan admired Rosemary, and when I told him that she was to be my guest for a few days, he not only arranged the

dinner party but roasted the duck for it. His and my memories of the event differ. I mostly remember how hard I
worked to get the always diffident and shy Haughton in
conversation with the merry but laconic Lonergan. Of the
conversation itself I remember only one thing: after a brief
exchange with Rosemary, Lonergan turned to Bill and said
that Rosemary had, in just a few minutes, sketched what it
had taken him a whole chapter of *Insight* (his *magnum
opus*) to do: she had described the uses of common sense,
one of the basic categories in Lonergan's cognitional theory—the same common sense she had used in her book to
bring abstract theological concepts home to us.

But since it's hard to find books like hers today, one of
the last places most of us look to for nourishing our spiritual lives is the reading of theology. I puzzle over this. Not
too long ago, from the forties through the seventies, say,
one did not need special training to understand and benefit
from much of the theology being done, including many of
the books I studied at Harvard. Reinhold Niebuhr's *The
Responsible Self* and Martin Buber's *I and Thou* were addressed to a broad readership, and were intended to be of
help to the layperson. After Vatican II and the theological
renewal accompanying it, my sisters and I read Catholic
theologians Hans Küng, Edward Schillebeeckx, and Bernard

Häring, and some of the essays of the German Jesuit Karl Rahner, even if we did not attempt his rigorous *Theological Investigations*.

Today the situation is more complex. The reading of much contemporary theology, with its highly specialized postmodern vocabularies and philosophical concepts, is hopelessly daunting for most of us. Theology has been virtually divorced from spirituality, and with its migration to the academy, it is practiced by many as a self-contained discipline, written largely by theologians for other theologians, not for the general reader like you and me. Here, as in other disciplines of the liberal arts curriculum (not the least literature), theory reigns supreme, and pretty abstruse theory at that.

Of course, there is a place for theory, for theories. But they are not meant for most of us, any more than advanced scientific or mathematical accounts in other disciplines are. Our problem is that there are not many "translators"—not many Rosemary Haughtons—who, like those in the sciences explaining how genetics accounts for the color of our eyes and chaos theory for a change in the weather, not only help make the theory intelligible to nonprofessionals but help us see its relationship to our lives as well. At the same time, we have a plethora of popular books on spirituality. But many of them are empty of serious theological consideration, floating like balloons above the religious landscape, unmoored from the beliefs of any tradition at all. Perhaps that is why I and other nuns that I have asked do not read books like Neale Donald Walsch's *Conversations with God*.

Of course, I read much more—what else does one do in graduate school but read? Günther Bornkamm's *Jesus of Nazareth* replaced Guardini's *The Lord* as my favorite book about Jesus. As the title indicates, the book accented Jesus' humanity and developed a "Christology from below," in contrast to Guardini's "Christology from above," with its starting point in the divinity of Christ. Here and in my studies of the Christian scriptures, I was introduced to what scholars call "the self-consciousness" of Jesus, the notion that he came gradually to a knowledge of himself and his mission, and was not born with the certainty of his divine nature, as I once believed. And it occurs to me now that reading must have played its part in his journey, as it does in ours.

When he came to Nazareth, where he had been brought up, he went to the synagogue on the sabbath day, as was his custom. He stood up to read, and the scroll of the prophet Isaiah was given to him. He unrolled the scroll and found the place where it was written: "The Spirit of the Lord is upon me, because he has anointed me to bring good news to the poor. He has sent me to proclaim release to the captives and recovery of sight to the blind, to let the oppressed go free, to proclaim the year of the Lord." . . . Then he began to say to them, "Today this scripture has been fulfilled in your hearing" (Luke 4:16ff).

We are not to imagine Jesus receiving knowledge of himself like a bolt out of the blue as he read the scripture out loud (he "found the place"). Rather, here he articulates what he was, no doubt, discovering in his own prayerful reading and study of the Hebrew scriptures, and taking a significant step in *appropriating* his identity as the Christ, the anointed one—his true self.

Because of what was going on in the world at the time, the two years I spent in Cambridge were especially exciting, if that is the word. I was a member of the HDS strike steering committee during the university-wide strike of 1969 in protest of the Vietnam War and ROTC on campus. As part of a delegation composed of faculty and students, I went to New York City to protest to David Rockefeller that money pledged to the Divinity School for building what is now Rockefeller Hall was tainted by Chase Manhattan's investments in South Africa. And I was among the group of students who met in Cronin's Bar on Mt. Auburn Street with Harvey Cox (HDS faculty member and author of the wildly popular *The Secular City*), and who were invited by the chaplain to Religious Experience Week at Colby College, during which the students occupied and "liberated" the chapel, and after which the chaplain was liberated from his job.

I mention all this, and with a certain humor, to give the flavor of the era, but as in the case of the Colby chaplain, it was not always fun or funny. Every time I raised my hand to vote on one or another issue in the endless "HDS community meetings" during the turmoil of the strike, I was in a state of moral crisis. What was the right thing to do? What did I really think? How much was I influenced by the way others were voting? By what they would think of the way I was voting? Hubert Jessup, a beautiful young man from California who always sat next to me in one of our classes and who was part of the Colby College delegation, was urging me to observe the strike and protest the war by not taking my end-term exams. I simply could not imagine myself explaining to Reverend Mother that I had lost a semester's credits for this reason. A short time after the strike I read Norman Mailer's 1968 *Armies of the Night*. The book recounts the travails of a factual-fictional character named Mailer participating in a Washington, D.C., protest against the Vietnam War. It brilliantly captured the kind of struggle that I had experienced—its foolishness, its pain, its conflict, its glory. It was, in other words, spiritual reading for me, not in offering solutions to the problems I had but in mirroring back to me my own confused moral being.

I was by this time, amid the changes taking place after Vatican II, freed from the stricture against secular reading. Sister Bridget and I—she is an Ursuline and a friend who began her doctoral studies in the English Department at Harvard in my second term—were careful to get permission not to wear the habit and for release from the rules of cloister, but I do not remember asking if I might read the Lord Peter Wimsey mysteries by Dorothy Sayers. I discovered them in the library of the Radcliffe Women's Graduate Dorm, where I lived my first semester, and devoured them. They were a feast for the imagination after so long a literary famine, presenting as they did not only well-constructed mysteries but also the deliciously tantalizing romance carried on from book to book between Lord Peter and the resistant Harriet Vane.

Eugene Peterson's annotated list of spiritual reading, *Take and Read*, names Dorothy Sayers's *The Man Born to Be King* but not the Lord Peter mysteries. He does, however, include Rex Stout's Nero Wolfe stories, making a case for detective Wolfe in his unmoving bulk as a parable for the church's uncompromising contemplative presence in the world. Even if that was what Stout—whom Peterson characterizes as "every bit as theologically perspicuous as [Jonathan] Swift"—intended, I don't know that we have to go so far to legitimize a book as good for the spirit. The reclusive orchid-tending Wolfe and his savvy legman Archie Goodwin have often lifted mine as I watched Archie trying to coax Nero to take on a case (usually because they need the money); as I walked familiar streets in Manhattan with Archie and drove up the Saw Mill River Parkway with him (an instance of that peculiar little pleasure we derive from stories set in locales we know); as the culprit, inveigled, somehow, to come to Wolfe's office, was confronted—and wit and justice triumphed again.

Reflection
PLEASURE: WASTING TIME
FOR THE SAKE OF GOD

H. L. Mencken's definition of puritanism: "the haunting fear that someone, somewhere, may be happy." Whether rooted in Protestant puritanism, in Roman Catholic Jansenism, or in that special brand of Jewish guilt, fear or suspicion of happiness, of pleasure, has cast a shadow over it in religious circles. Unfortunately, at least in the mainline denominations, Jewish and Christian, we associate religion and spirituality almost exclusively with asceticism, duty, hard work, suffering, earnestness of purpose, solemnity, and only occasionally with gladness, delight. I often look around in church at the utterly expressionless faces singing "Alleluia! Alleluia!" and wonder why we don't let our faces know what our lips are saying. And I think of the Hasidim with their joyful dancing and of our black brothers and sisters at worship in some pentecostal churches; they smile, clap their hands, stamp their feet, their bodies swaying to the rhythm of the music. They seem to be having a good time—and in church, heaven forbid!

But listen to this favorite passage of mine from Augustine's *Confessions*, its sensuous delight in the love of God contradicting our misconceptions:

What is it that I love when I love my God? . . . It is a certain light that I love and melody and fragrance and embrace that I love when I love my God—a light, melody, fragrance, food, embrace of the God-within, where, for my soul, that shines which space does not contain; that sounds which time

does not sweep away; that is fragrant which the
breeze does not dispel; and that tastes sweet which,
fed upon, is not diminished; and that clings close
which no satiety disparts—this is what I love when
I love my God.

According to the saint, moreover, pleasure is to be found
among the greatest of human goods: *frui,* the Latin for "to
enjoy," he says, is the sole occupation of the blessed in
heaven, rather than its opposite: *uti,* "to use."

And it is this kind of nonutilitarian attitude that characterizes communal worship at its best, according to Romano Guardini in his classic *The Spirit of the Liturgy.*

The soul must learn to abandon, at least in prayer,
the restlessness of purposeful activity; it must learn
to waste time for the sake of God. . . . It must learn
not to be continually yearning to do something, to
attack something, to accomplish something useful,
but to play the divinely ordained game of the
liturgy in liberty and beauty and holy joy before God.

Except when we turn in worship to pray for people, things,
events, as we may legitimately do, its primary purpose is

the contemplation, appreciation, and praise of Goodness, Truth, Beauty, Holiness, Love. It is its own *raison d'être*.

In fact, Ignatius of Loyola derived the notions of consolation, a kind of spiritual pleasure, and its opposite, desolation, from an experience of reading, the occasion of his conversion. When the high-living and vainglorious courtier Iñigo of Loyola was recovering from a leg wound received in the battle of Pamplona, he found in the house of the friend with whom he was staying a life of Christ and several lives of the saints. With nothing else to do, he read them. And he noted that while the reading of frivolous romances wasted his spirit, and left him dry and lethargic, these books energized him, filled him up. Thus it was that Iñigo, in a conversion not unlike Augustine's, and certainly in another instance of book providence, started on the path to becoming the Ignatius we know, "a soldier of Christ," dedicated *ad majoram Dei gloriam*, the motto of the Jesuits.

Beyond prayer, in a spirituality that embraces our whole lives, pleasure has its rightful place. It need not and should not be thought of as time out from our relationship with God, or only as a kind of gas station where we fill up our tanks in order to get to the next "important" thing we have to do. As Virginia Woolf notes in the essay "How One Should Read a Book":

Yet who reads to bring about an end, however desirable? Are there not some pursuits that we practice because they are good in themselves, and some pleasures that are final? And is this not among them? I have sometimes dreamt, at least, that when the Day of Judgment dawns and the great conquerors and lawyers and statesmen come to receive their rewards—their crowns, their laurels, their names carved indelibly upon imperishable marble— the Almighty will turn to Peter and will say, not without a certain envy when he sees us coming with our books under our arms, "Look, these need no reward. We have nothing to give them here. They have loved reading."

It is a nice conceit; and I do find reading heavenly. But it would be a sour God who would deny us pleasure in heaven or here on earth. And it would be a stingy Creator who did not wish us to share in the divine enchantment at the creation: "God saw everything that he had made, and indeed, it was very good" (Genesis 1: 31). And who did not share that creativity with the artists among us, also for our enjoyment.

So we read for pleasure, and we find it in all sorts of ways. We love stories, and have since we were children;

they satisfy our need to know "how things turn out," our desire for completion. Humorous writing (very hard to do, I think) makes us laugh. Our appetite for knowledge and information is painlessly gratified, especially, but not only, in biography and historical fiction. We travel to different lands without leaving home. We note the apt observation, the pithy phrase. We are arrested by beautiful prose, its cadences and rhythm. The design and scope of the great literary works that embrace whole worlds, both within and without, astonish us.

Our pleasures are, no doubt, as varied as our individual interests and taste. I can't even catalogue, let alone explain, my own. But here is a sampling of them. Though I read it years ago, I still remember Nadine Gordimer's description of a bull standing in a field as "lustful but bored." It is both funny—people laugh when I repeat it to them—and telling. In three words she perfectly captures the mindless vacant nature of animal sexuality, so different from our own, which, if it does nothing else for us when aroused, at least gets our attention. (That's probably why the phrase strikes us as funny.)

In Sue Grafton's alphabet mysteries, I look forward to meeting private investigator Kinsey Millhone the way I look forward to meeting an old friend whose idiosyncratic and sometimes contradictory habits I know well. In the next book, she will, I'm sure, go out on her early-morning two-mile jog, like a health nut, only later in the day to indulge in a peanut butter and pickle sandwich, or a bowl of "milk of tomato" soup and a gooey, grilled Velveeta cheese sandwich. She won't have a proper dress to wear to a ritzy social occasion. She'll come home at night, glad to be alone in the snug little carriage house that she rents from her interesting, good-looking, eighty-six-year-old neighbor Henry. And somehow, without tiring her fans, Grafton will weave enough of Millhone's past life and loves into the story of the latest case to acquaint the new reader with a fully developed character—no small feat.

Among the many delights in Tom Wolfe's *Bonfire of the Vanities*, I found the kind of intellectual pleasure that mathematicians must experience in the elegance of a simple equation. Young Wall Street millionaire Sherman McCoy—"the Master of the Universe," he thought—is driving back to Manhattan from Kennedy Airport, his mistress Maria with him in his Mercedes. In a single event on which the plot depends, he takes the wrong exit off the Triborough Bridge in New York City. Instead of bringing him home to his plush Park Avenue apartment, it leads him into another universe altogether, the *Bronx!* Where he has an accident . . . involving a young black man! Which lands him for the first of many times in the Bronx Criminal Courts Building! By the end of the book, no longer Master of the Universe, he is "a career defendant," barely able to pay the rent for his two rooms in an East Thirty-fourth Street high-rise. That wrong turn has changed his life. But it has also given Wolfe a large canvas on which to paint, with great comic/satiric brio, the hugely discrepant social realities and the colorfully venal residents of two boroughs in this fantastic but maddening city. A simple authorial device: one city plus one bridge equals two universes. Elegant.

Finally, in this very short catalogue, here is a favorite instance of the long-acknowledged "joy of recognition" that reading affords us. It is the joy that comes from recognizing something about ourselves, or others, or life, that we have vaguely known but never "said" to ourselves so clearly. Already at the end of the first chapter of *Middlemarch*, I, a younger sister and a nun with a vow of obedience, knew the author to be a wise woman. Summing up an encounter between its principal character, Dorothea Brooke, and Celia, her younger sister, George Eliot observes, "Since they could remember, there had always been a mixture of criticism and awe in the attitude of Celia's mind towards her elder sister." That's me! I said, enabled to recognize and own—"own up to"—a part of myself when I saw it in Celia. Then Eliot continues: "The younger had always worn a yoke; but is there any yoked creature without its private opinions?" I love that last clause, more as a reminder of life in the convent in the old days than of me as a sibling. I still find in it the joy of recognizing a truth about the human condition itself, and myself as just one of many who were or are in thrall to another. Eliot does all of this in two sentences, a succinct example of one of the ways that literature can crystallize our knowledge of ourselves at the same time that it enlarges our sympathies.

In good novels, and I count *Middlemarch* among the best I have read, we can find pleasure—I do—in the close observation and insightful portrayal of human personalities, the complexity of our relationships, the ambiguity of our motives, the immense power inherent in social structures to influence our lives, the forces that are arrayed against the human good. And I taste the rightness of Wayne Booth's statement in *The Rhetoric of Fiction:* "There is a pleasure from learning the simple truth, and there is a pleasure from learning that the truth is not simple." The latter is a strange pleasure, isn't it? We are satisfied, somehow, because, even though we might wish it otherwise, that's most often the truth about truth—including the truth about ourselves. It's a lesson we have to learn over and over. Those who do not learn it, like fundamentalists of all stripes, for example, can do a lot of harm.

RECOVERING THE SELF

Stories: Facts and Fiction

W HEN, IN MY MID-FORTIES, I began to
realize what the experience of conversion and finding one's true self might mean, I thought with some pique:
It's not fair. You spend your whole life becoming who you
are only to find out that you have to change, radically. I
imagined that I myself and not God's grace could effect
the change. Later, after some rough bumps and perilous
detours in my spiritual journey, I remember thinking that I
had lost my way, that the plot of my life story had been ob-
scured. It had begun well enough: the bright teenager winning a scholarship to a Catholic high school!, which led her
to a Catholic college and to the convent. Graduate studies

brought me, after some delay, in my thinking, to teaching at the college, where I imagined that someday I might become superior of the community, as my sister novices had predicted of me. That is not the way the story unfolded. God was going to do for me what I could not do for myself. My version of my life was not God's version. I was not who I thought I was.

I never could, by dint of my own efforts, have changed myself the way life changed me, the way God's love wanted me to change. "Love in action is a harsh and dreadful thing compared to love in dreams," as the monk Zossima says in *The Brothers Karamazov*. Or as Russian Orthodox Archbishop Anthony Bloom says in his superb little book *Beginning to Pray*, "To meet God means to enter the cage of a tiger—it is not a pussycat that you meet— it's a tiger. The realm of God is dangerous. You must enter into it and not just seek information about it." I entered the cage of the tiger and felt that I was being flayed, the word I applied to myself even before I knew exactly what it meant. I had to look it up in the dictionary to find that it means "to strip off the skin or the surface of, to strip of possessions," in my case all the notions of position and influence in which my ego had layered itself.

Having completed the work for my master of theological studies degree in December 1969, I left Harvard to begin teaching at the College of New Rochelle in the January term, 1970. Already, during my last term at HDS, there had been signs of the frightening depression that I was to undergo after my first semester at the college. It had begun with feelings of unease and melancholy, and progressed in the following year to a loss of energy for or interest in anything, combined with restlessness and acute anxiety. If you have not experienced depression and think it is like sadness, or the blues, or a passing bad mood, you are wrong. It is a different creature altogether, a huge, shapeless, smothering, gray beast that allows you not a moment's peace. And although my depression was awful enough for me, it was not as deep as some I know of; I never, for instance, missed a class. A year of therapy and prescriptions for Doriden for insomnia, Valium for anxiety, and Elavil, a mood elevator, brought me out of mine, and I hope never to visit that bleak land again. Although the doctor had said I should probably stay on the Elavil, I discontinued it but kept using the Doriden and the Valium. At the time, I was as ignorant as everybody else of the addictive power of both.

The CNR that I returned to as a faculty member in 1970 was, like many other Catholic colleges and universities then, in turmoil. Lay teachers were beginning to object to the oligarchic governance of the nuns and to demand a voice in decision making. Men's Catholic colleges, such as Fordham and Holy Cross, had begun to admit women, reducing the pool of students for women's colleges. New legislation about money for higher education in New York State was requiring Catholic colleges to demonstrate that they were not proselytizing. Crucifixes were taken down from classroom walls, and in a thoroughgoing revision of the curriculum at CNR, courses in religious studies were no longer required but elective. Over a period of several years, that department was reduced by half. My contract was not renewed for the fall 1973 term. It was a blow, a staggering blow. Sister Dorothy Ann, president of the college at the time, offered me a position on the campus ministry team there, but that did not seem to me to make full use of my theological training. And so, with the blessing of my superiors (Vatican II had brought us freedom in choice of ministry), I returned to Cambridge in hope of finding new work.

And by a stroke of what I thought of as "book providence"—an instance, in this case, of being directed by reading to what I was meant to do with my life—I did find it. I had read several interesting and challenging articles about religion and higher education in *Commonweal* by Myron B. Bloy, Jr. The ideas they expressed about the need to integrate our religious and intellectual lives, in-

stead of compartmentalizing them, as we often do, intrigued me. At a time when we were all being urged to "get
in touch with our feelings," I wanted to ask people, "Are
you in touch with your *thoughts?*" believing then, as I do
now, that what we *think* about the world, ourselves, and
God plays as important a part in our spiritual lives as our
feelings do. (Do we think, for instance, that we are the *only*
"chosen people," whether as Jews, Catholics, Muslims—
or Americans? Does such thinking enlarge our spirits?
What are the consequences of it for others? And what kind
of God does it manifest?)

From the blurbs in the articles, I knew that Bloy was an
Episcopal priest, and that the Church Society for College
Work, of which he was the director, was located in Cambridge. One day when I was visiting Bridget, the nun who
had joined me at Harvard in my second semester, and who
was at this time living in a graduate apartment on Brattle
Street, I looked up CSCW in the telephone directory. It
was housed at the Episcopal Theological Seminary (now
the Episcopal Divinity School) in the very next set of
buildings from where I was at that moment. Taking this as
a good omen, and wanting to meet this man whose ideas
were so attractive to me, even though I might not find a
job, I'm not sure that I called for an appointment. I walked
over to the seminary, introduced myself to Mike, as Bloy

was called, volunteered my services for a semester, and was hired the next. It seemed providential to me at the time, and still does. And it all began (and continued to unfold) with reading those articles.

This marked another turning point in my life journey. CSCW was an ecumenically Christian organization devoted to the research and development of resources for campus ministers and faculty concerned with the part that communities of faith can play in our colleges and universities. Working now with adults and as the generalist that I am rather than the disciplinary specialist that I am not, I found my métier. And Mike, a vital, engaging man, intellectually curious, with a tough-minded faith, became a mentor. When he was made executive director of the interreligious (Protestants, Catholics, Jews) National Institute for Campus Ministries (NICM) in 1975, he brought me along as Northeast regional director.

Now what had seemed like an abrupt and disappointing about-face when I left CNR turned instead into an ever larger and more enriching circle. If my stay at Harvard had widened my acquaintance with Protestants, both personally and in my reading, my work at NICM brought me for the first time in my life into close contact with Jews and to a new understanding of Judaism. I met a Jewish rabbi younger than I was who as a kid had been beaten up on Good Friday in the Bronx. I worked with Arthur Waskow, read his *Godwrestling;* with Arthur Green, author of *Tormented Master: A Life of Rabbi Nahman of Bratslav;* with Paul van Buren, a friend of Mike's, whose work-in-progress on what was to become *A Theology of the Jewish-Christian Reality* had moved Mike to insist that NICM include Jews.

Although the Vatican II document *Nostra aetate* had articulated a new understanding of the relationship between Catholicism and the other world religions, especially Judaism, that understanding hadn't yet come home to me. It was these books and these people that changed my ideas about who I was as a Catholic. I had to revise my thinking about Jesus, to realize the fullness of his Jewishness, the Jewishness of his own spirituality, and that his mission was not to convert Jews to another religion but to call them to fidelity to their own covenant with God. I understood that Christians, far from supplanting the Jews as God's chosen people, are privileged to share in their everlasting covenant. Because if that covenant is not everlasting, if God is not faithful to the Jews, then we're all in big trouble, Jews and Christians alike. These insights, along with an increasing number of books about the Holocaust

and the part that Christians played in it, as witnessed to by
books like Anne Frank's heartbreakingly young and hope-
ful diary and Elie Wiesel's stark *Night*, changed forever
my understanding of and attitude toward Jews. My Catholic
self was becoming, thank God, catholic.

The work at NICM was broadening, challenging, satisfying. I traveled to conferences we both sponsored and
attended, sat up late into the night with the guys—I was
the only woman on the staff—unwinding, talking, drinking. Exciting as life there was, however, Mike and I, for
different reasons, left NICM in 1978. He became the chaplain at Sweet Briar College in Virginia; I became director
of the Ursuline Retreat Center in Beacon, New York, at
the site of our former novitiate. I was experiencing what I
thought (in a self-aggrandizing way) was a "dark night of
the soul," that purification reserved by John of the Cross
for those called to the higher mystical states. Prayer was
difficult, if not impossible, for me, and I imagined that ex-
changing the hectic, pressured life I was leading at NICM
for the peace and relative solitude of Beacon would solve
my problem. It did not. Even with all the time in the world
at my disposal, the silence, and the beauty of the surround-
ing mountains, I remained desolate of spirit. I left Beacon
for a convent in the Bronx, did a little writing and some

part-time teaching, and worked for a short period at a publishing house.

In 1983, Mike, still pursuing his vision of an authentically integrated religious and intellectual life, founded the Association for Religion and Intellectual Life (ARIL). He volunteered his services as director and editor of its journal *Religion and Intellectual Life,* all the while serving full-time at Sweet Briar. Shortly after his sad, sudden, and premature death in 1985, I, who had been merely a member of the ARIL board and book review editor for the journal, was asked to take his place. With very little training or experience, I became an editor and temporary director of ARIL's programs. Five years later, at my initiative, *Religion and Intellectual Life* merged with the well-known, long-established *Cross Currents,* where along with Joe Cunneen and Bill Birmingham, I served as coeditor until 1997. From Joe and Bill, both consummately skilled editors, I finally learned what I was doing.

Those are the facts of my life as they would appear on my résumé, or even as they did appear to my sisters and family at the time. True, the facts might signal that my religious/intellectual horizons had been broadened, and that my thinking had been changed in ways meaningful to my spiritual life. I acknowledge that. But during the years

1975–83, I experienced a kind of dark night different from the one John of the Cross had in mind, even though, in God's mercy, it had the same purifying effect. Circling back over the same path that we just covered in the literary labyrinth that I'm tracing in this book, I will tell you now another story about what was happening to me at this time. It will not appear on my résumé, but it is no less factual.

Alarmed by Barbara Gordon's *I'm Dancing As Fast As I Can*, which had not only a good bit of information about Valium, but especially a vivid autobiographical account of the effects the drug had on Gordon, I had identified her symptoms in myself, and had quit taking it cold turkey when I moved to Beacon. But I replaced the drug with more alcohol than I had been drinking in my NICM days, until I could not go without it for even a single day. I was becoming, I feared, an alcoholic. I didn't talk to anyone about my fear, but I took the tests for detecting the disease in magazines at the dentist's and doctor's offices. And I secretly read a copy of the book *Alcoholics Anonymous* that I found in the convent library; I don't remember what I thought of it. I didn't stop drinking.

Alcoholism—still not very well understood by our society—is, as I learned later, a physical, mental (including emotional), and spiritual disease. It affected every part of my life—my mental capacities, including my judgment, my work, and my relationships with family, friends, sisters, and colleagues, and with God. My spirit was dying, dead. During the last several years of my drinking, I could neither pray nor read for any length of time, having lost the power of concentration required by both. I remember only one book from this time of my life; it was written by a hermit, but I can't recall either its title or its author. As the disease progressed, I became filled with hopelessness, self-loathing, and shame. My life of self-indulgence and deceit was so far from the dreams of heroic sanctity I had had for myself as a young nun.

Finally, in January 1983, after a terrible struggle in which I promised myself, daily, not to drink again and failed, daily, I acknowledged that I was powerless over alcohol. I saw a nun who was an alcoholism counselor, told my superior of her recommendation that I get inpatient treatment, and was immediately sent to a twenty-eight-day rehab. Very few of my relatives or friends, or the nuns, knew of my alcoholism; when I called my sister (my mother had died the year before) to tell her where I was going, she was stunned. Just before we hung up she said, "This took more courage than when Granny left the old country to come over here."

All of this was a humiliating defeat for my false self, and an amazingly grace-filled birth of a new self, humbled, chastened, scared. But one does not achieve mental/emotional and spiritual sobriety, much less serenity, immediately upon "putting down the drink." Nor did I recover my interest in reading immediately. In the early days of my sobriety when, no longer sedated by alcohol, I couldn't sleep, I read *Alcoholics Anonymous*, this time with a fierce intensity. Although the first part of it gives some medical information about the disease of alcoholism, practical advice about dealing with it, and a description of the now famous Twelve Steps, two-thirds of the book is devoted to the stories of recovering alcoholics, all told in the first person. I read those stories over and over again. I could manage them. They were short, clearly written. With titles like "The Vicious Cycle," "Fear of Fear," "Belle of the Bar," they told of the ravages that the disease had wrought upon the authors. In fact, the more desperate and sordid the stories—some very different from my own—the more hope they gave me that I too could recover. More important, they had the power, as stories do, of compelling me to identify with the *feelings* of the people in them, feelings of helplessness, remorse, sadness, and fear. Whether they were written by a high-living New York socialite or a Bowery bum, I recognized myself in these stories, recognized the authors as just like me, regardless of their social status, race, educational background—a more valuable spiritual lesson than I realized at the time.

Then, so early in my recovery, I altogether missed even the explicitly spiritual component in every story. But if I had to characterize the book now, regardless of where you find it in the bookstores, I wouldn't call it a self-help book. Neither would I classify it as "inspirational," which sounds to me too ethereal to convey the life-and-death struggle—a physical, mental, and spiritual struggle for their very bodies, minds, and souls—that alcoholics are engaged in. It is most often found in the "recovery" sections of bookstores, and that's fine with me if it helps people to find it. But because recovery really means salvation here, and because the book gives such down-to-earth and wise spiritual counsel, I would call it spiritual reading, plain and simple. It's a marvel to me that only four years after the beginning of A.A. in 1935, when there were only about one hundred members in the fellowship, the founders recognized how important it was to have a book that would carry the message of A.A.'s program ("It's a spiritual program," A.A. members openly say). And that they were wise enough to realize that telling stories, in print and in person, was the most powerful vehicle for doing it.

Again I learned, not from my doctor but from reading

another life story, Donald Spoto's biography of Tennessee Williams, *The Kindness of Strangers* (Spoto taught in the religious studies department at CNR when I was there), something else about myself. In the book he describes the addictive power of the drug Doriden and the devastating effects it had on the playwright, causing sluggishness, faulty judgment, irritability, moroseness. For what it's worth, I believe now that my addiction to alcohol began with the Doriden I took for insomnia when I had TB, and that I continued taking for years afterward. I think it caused my depression, whence the Valium. I have, without doubt, an addictive personality, but I was started down the bitter path to alcoholism by prescription drugs. No shame, especially back then, in a nun taking prescription drugs.

And finally, fiction. Malcolm Lowry's novel *Under the Volcano* was first published in 1947. Rich in symbolism and mythical and literary references, it can, like T. S. Eliot's *The Waste Land*, be read as emblematic of the spiritual crisis of the modern world—in this instance, however, as seen through the portrayal of its hero, or antihero, "the Consul," a drunk.

We first hear from Geoffrey Firmin, a former British consul in Mexico, in "a letter of sorts, though one that the writer undoubtedly had little intention, possibly no capability for the further tactile effort, of posting." Written to his former wife, Yvonne, it begins, ". . . Night: and once again, the mighty grapple with death." Against the background noise of "the daemonic orchestras" of the DTs and "the howling pariah dogs of Mexico," it introduces, before we meet him, a "great explorer who has discovered some extraordinary land from which he can never return to give his knowledge to the world: but the name of this land is hell. It is not Mexico of course but in the heart."

This is the author, Lowry, himself an alcoholic, telling us what he is attempting, and defying his own words, brilliantly succeeds at in the book. The setting for the story is Mexico, its natural grandeur, its volcanoes and mountains, its abysses, the glories of its past and its present political humiliation, and poverty, and tawdriness. The hell, the land of alcoholism, is in the heart of the Consul. And we explore it in terrifying detail: the awful loneliness; the deceit; the desperation; the remorse and self-loathing. We endure with him the agonizing wait in the morning for the first bar to open, in evening dress but with no socks; the shakes; the hallucinations; the falls; the blackouts. We experience the fleeting moments, when just drunk enough, but not too drunk, of gaiety, of lucidity. As the book progresses and Yvonne returns in hope of bringing back to life the genuine love that she and Geoff still share, we watch the disintegration of a human person, of a self who knows *no se puede vivir sin amar* (one cannot live without loving). And who cannot not "choose" the next drink instead, aware all the while of what he is doing.

I knew that land, not, by the grace of God, in the physical and mental devastation of advanced alcoholism like the Consul's, but in its spiritual desolation. It is hell. And even though I read the book with a deep sense of relief and gratitude for my own deliverance, Lowry's meticulous account of the double consciousness, of the helpless and hopeless soul-rotting inauthenticity of the active alcoholic, overwhelmed my gratitude. As good, serious fiction can, it disclosed to me, more vividly, more accurately, more articulately than my own memories, what my experience had been.

Reflecting on the book now, however, I'm filled, rather, with an icy astonishment. That the author, caught in the throes of this disease, was enough in command of his faculties to write the book is already cause for wonder. More astonishing to me is the thought of him, with a triple consciousness, as it were, standing outside of himself, observing and recording the doubleness, the devastation and despair that were, most certainly, his own, and even jauntily at times. It is the jauntiness that chills me. It evidences the most nihilistic kind of whistling in the dark, nihilistic because it knows, for sure, that finally the whistler will plunge into the abyss. The Consul dies drunk at the end of the book, its last sentence, "Somebody threw a dead dog after him into the ravine." Lowry died at age fifty-six from an overdose of barbiturates and alcohol.

Do you have to be an alcoholic to read and understand this book—to appreciate its mastery, the brilliance of its prose, to grieve at its account of a lost soul? No, of course not. "Fundamentally *Under the Volcano* is no more *about* alcoholism than *King Lear* is *about* senility," says Stephen Spender. To think one would have to be an alcoholic would undermine the power and value of many of the books we read, about things that, like alcoholism—or the Holocaust—we hope we will never have to experience. Should we read them? Yes. Here is what Kafka, in characteristically extreme fashion, wrote in a letter to his friend Oskar Pollak about books like these:

> Altogether, I think we ought to read only books that bite and sting us. If the book we are reading doesn't shake us awake like a blow on the skull, why bother reading it in the first place? So that it can make us happy, as you put it? Good God, we'd be just as happy if we had no books at all; books

that make us happy we could, in a pinch, also write ourselves. What we need are books that hit us like a most painful misfortune, like the death of someone we loved more than we love ourselves, that make us feel as though we had been banished to the woods, far from any human presence, like a suicide. A book must be the axe for the frozen sea within us. That is what I believe.

I thank God that I'm not Kafka, or Lowry. But I know something of frozen seas. And so do you.

In the years since 1983, I have been in recovery, never cured, with every kind of support in fellowship and from God that I could ask for—and this is where I always hope to be. It is a blessed state to be in, to know myself in. Recovery is the perfect metaphor—though it is a reality—for the never-ending adventure of finding, in my very woundedness and weakness and sinfulness, "the face I had before my parents were born," my true self. Gaining freedom little by little from the tyranny of a self-regarding ego, I am coming to know myself as a creature among creatures in a vast cosmos, a child of God among other children, dearly loved by Jesus, and empowered by the Spirit to find and do God's will. The book *Twelve Steps and Twelve Traditions* says it simply and soberly, reminding me of St. Thérèse's "little way," and what Buddhists call "the ordinary mind" or "beginner's mind." It offers as good a description of spirituality as any I've read elsewhere, and as good as you are going to find in this book on a spirituality of reading:

> Service, gladly rendered, obligations squarely met, trouble well accepted or solved with God's help, the knowledge that at home or in the world outside we are partners in a common effort, the well-understood fact that in God's sight all human beings are important, the proof that love freely given surely brings a full return, the certainty that we are no longer isolated in self-constructed prisons, the surety that we need no longer be square pegs in round holes but can fit and belong in God's scheme of things—these are the permanent and legitimate satisfactions of right living for which no amount of pomp and circumstance, no heap of material possessions, could possibly be substitutes. True ambition is not what we thought it was. True ambition is the desire to live usefully and walk humbly under the grace of God.

Is this, then, what I have been looking for in all the reading that I have done? The "meaning of life," a portrayal of who I am called to be? I believe it is. For once, the truth *is* simple. Simple to state, not easy to achieve. But that's another matter.

Reflection
THE GRAMMAR OF THE SPIRIT

It was during the late eighties, I think, several years after I had fully recovered my ability to concentrate for long periods of time, that the thought occurred to me: Life is short. Why spend it reading only currently popular books, most of them destined to be forgotten? And so I set myself to reading the classic novels that I had missed out on during the periods of my literary cloister and my drinking. Without any system at all, in no particular order, and over a period of years, I read (some of) Jane Austen, Charles Dickens, Anthony Trollope, Henry James, George Eliot, Edith Wharton, Dostoevsky, Tolstoy, Willa Cather, Virginia Woolf, and James Joyce.

I'm glad, really, that I read these authors in my maturity. With more knowledge and experience of life, I was better able to appreciate them. By that time I had done enough writing myself (short articles only, and never fiction) to realize how hard it is to write clearly, let alone to invent a structure that will support a dramatic arc, tell a story in a compelling way. And I had the patience and perseverance to deal with prose that, on the whole, is more formal, more ornate, and more complex than that of many contemporary authors, and, in the case of James, for instance, much more difficult to follow. I wondered, and still do, whether something has happened to our language that diminishes our ability to read these books. It couldn't be that their thousands of readers in the past whose esteem raised them to the status of classics in the first place were smarter than we are. Did they possess a linguistic capacity that we just do not have?

Now, I don't want to appear curmudgeonly about this point. I acknowledge that in the matter of language, as in other domains, what is at stake may largely be a question of taste, or age—or both. (I confess that I have always preferred Grand Central, even before its restoration, to the poor boring Penn Station that modernism gave us; my eye wants scope, ornament, color. And Debussy, Duke Ellington, and Rodgers and Hammerstein to Philip Glass, the Rolling Stones, and Andrew Lloyd Weber; my ear needs interesting harmony and melody—whatever happened to melody?) I seem, when I am reading, without even knowing that I'm doing it, to look for grace and rhythm in prose. Which is why, at one point, I couldn't read the mostly minimalist authors like Bobbie Ann Mason that *The New Yorker* was publishing. It wasn't plot or character development that I missed, or even that I didn't perceive the plain speech of the *dramatis personae* as true to the way they, and maybe we, talk. But as these stories stylistically out-Hemingwayed Hemingway, I couldn't bear the relentless beat of the short simple declarative sentences, marching one after another in the narrative, like prisoners in a chain gang, when my spirit was longing for the fluid "grammar" of Fred Astaire and Ginger Rogers, twirling, dipping, tapping, gliding.

And I say "my spirit" on purpose, because I believe that language, in all its dimensions, articulates the human spirit. Language is grammatically complex because we are, our thoughts and feelings and relationships are, because life is. We don't experience ourselves, or life, simply, declaratively. We need subordinate clauses, compound-complex sentences to express the reality of who we are, to show what is more important or less important, *just how* one thought or feeling or situation is related to another.

And we need a rich palette of words, with their different, fine shades of meaning, from which to select just the right word. Surely these are among the blessings that good prose and poetry, without trying to say everything or saying too much, bestow on us. They find the words, find the grammar, to convey "what oft was thought, but ne'er so well expressed," as Alexander Pope said. Thus, to the extent that our language, both literary and spoken, is monochromatic, monorhythmic, grammatically unarticulated, sometimes monosyllabic—impoverished and flattened—so are our spirits. "I mean, y'know, like . . ." Yes, like what, exactly? I want to say. And they are certainly impoverished if we can't claim the treasures of our literary heritage as our own.

ALONE AT THE CENTER?

Intimacy in Reading and Prayer

Reading is an intimate act," claimed author Harold Brodkey, "perhaps more intimate than any other human act. I say this because of the prolonged (or intense) exposure of one mind to another." Virginia Woolf was more specific: "At the heart of the pleasure of reading," she said, "is the delight in a free union, like a very intimate conversation or an act of love" (word and flesh again). Reading, though usually a solitary act, *is* a conversation, a complex exchange between oneself and the author (Can I trust you?), the characters in the book (Oh, Anna Karenina, don't be so foolish!), with oneself (I've felt that way). It is also, as reader/response theorists have taught us, a conversation with the community of readers to which we belong, with the interpretations we inherit from others, of Hamlet, say, as the melancholy Dane (Do I "read" him that way?).

When not done alone but with another person, reading can also be a vehicle for greater intimacy between the readers, all the while enlarging their world. Two long-married couples I know have been reading books out loud to each other for years. Tony Stoneburner reads while Pat prepares dinner; Joe and Sally Cunneen read at bedtime, working through over a period of months something as long and complicated as *War and Peace*. They do not call it spiritual reading, but I would. Sally says that:

> the night readings are quiet times that prepare us for sleep by making a break with other concerns. What this reading provides is a continuity to our lives that we share no matter what else is happening in "real" life. When things are somewhat scattered and hectic, the reading calms us down physically and at the same time pulls us imaginatively and emotionally into African villages and nineteenth-century French or Russian drawing rooms.... (There are always some wise phrases that stick with us and funny lines we can use in

public as a private language. . . .) In the long run, getting to know all the characters and their stories by reading them to one another vastly extends the range of our human acquaintance, and at the same time helps us accept the limits of the human condition.

Even if you have never done this kind of reading, haven't you felt the joy of finding a kindred spirit merely on discovering that someone else loves the books that you love? Or wouldn't you like to talk to the stranger on the subway reading a favorite book of yours? You have an urge to tell her how much you enjoyed it and why; you want her to prize it as much you do. And you hope that she does. You desire, if only for a moment, to experience the kind of book kinship that some cities are fostering with the suggestion that readers wear a button to signal a book they want to talk about, giving them "permission" for this peculiarly intimate kind of conversation.

With all of this, however, finally, reading is a keenly personal act. Each of us—even Sally and Joe—reads a book against the template of his own personality, experience, tastes, and dispositions at the moment, so that in a very real way each reader is the cocreator of the work being read; it is not a one-sided affair. And it is not as if nothing were being asked of us. A kind of asceticism is required, at least in serious reading. As we try to be in the important and meaningful relationships in our lives, we can be generous, attentive partners, open to and accepting of a way of being in the world different from our own. Or we can be selfish, greedy, lazy, unwilling to give the time, the concentration, the sympathy that a book—or a friend—might ask of us, unwilling, sometimes unable, to give of ourselves or receive of others. This is what intimacy is, isn't it, a mutual giving and receiving of selves? And I think that it is more easily come by in books, especially in fiction, than in life.

In fiction, we have virtual access to a character's inner life, and in varying ways. From the viewpoint of the omniscient author, we can know more about a character than the character knows herself, and as in Henry James's *Portrait of a Lady,* we are brought to see the harm that such ignorance brings to its protagonist, in this case Isabel Archer, and to those around her.

In *Ulysses,* James Joyce's breakthrough to the literary device of stream of consciousness, we are made privy to Dubliner Leopold Bloom's interiority, to the entire conversation he has with himself in the course of a single day, June 16. We are hearing, overhearing, really, the thoughts that spring spontaneously, randomly to Bloom's mind;

they mirror most of the conversations we have with our-selves, carried on without a great deal of reflection or self-consciousness, as was Joyce's intention. Like Bloom, we most often don't hear what we are saying to ourselves and sometimes not even what we are saying to others. ("Nancy! Do you *hear* what you are saying?" my therapist used to ask me.) So that when we overhear Bloom's meanderings with the aesthetic distance that a work of art provides, we not only have better access to his interiority than he does, but we even have better access than usual to our own.

It is preeminently in Shakespeare, according to Harold Bloom's *Shakespeare: The Invention of the Human,* that char-acters do just this, "*overhear* themselves talking, whether to themselves or to others. Self-overhearing is their royal road to individuation," to becoming intimate with who they are, and then being able to change. (Isn't this the point of therapy also, owning oneself, and either accepting one-self—and others—or changing that self?) Bloom further says, "Shakespeare will go on explaining us, in part be-cause he invented us"—especially in Hamlet, the most fully individuated of characters, in Bloom's judgment.

This is a large claim to make for a single author, and I am not equipped to argue with it or defend it. But I realize that it is, in a way, the same claim that I am making for lit-erature as a whole in this spirituality of reading. We are who we are in part because of the literary tradition we inhabit. Whether we are aware of it or not, that tradition— including Shakespeare—has given us the very words we use to express ourselves (from the Latin *exprimere,* meaning "to press out, to mold or form one thing in imitation of another"). More deeply, if we are readers, literature, with its power to "get inside" us, to articulate our thoughts and feelings for us, affects our interiority. As we become intimate with the interiority of others in this privileged fashion, and if we are reflective, we may become more intimate with ourselves, "overhear" ourselves, and, however subtly, for better or for worse, depending on what we read, we may be changed.

But then the question arises, When do we reach the goal of our journey, the true self? Is it, as one interpretation of walking the labyrinth has it, when we reach the center of its circuitous path, from which we proceed outward to communion with others? And if that is true, are we alone at the center? These are the questions asked in Nadine Gordimer's superb *None to Accompany Me,* which I have read three times now, each time with greater insight into it and into myself.

The book takes its title from the second of two epigraphs it carries, a two-line poem by the seventeenth-century Japanese poet Basho: "None to accompany me on this path: / Nightfall in Autumn." Early on in the novel, the author tells us this about the protagonist, an aging white woman named Vera Stark: "For a long time—how many years?—Vera still told her husband everything. Or thought she did." (How deft a statement of the "devices and desires" of the heart, the title of one of P. D. James's novels, borrowed from the *Book of Common Prayer*.) In the unfolding of the book, with its plot and subplots embedded in the political reality of post-apartheid South Africa and within a cluster of images—clasped hands, a headless nude sculpture of her done by her husband, an old photograph, houses, housing, homes, the homeland (Vera works for a foundation that settles legal disputes over land owner-ship)—Vera discovers things about herself that she has not told herself; she becomes intimate with "herself, a final form of company discovered."

By the last chapter, freed by her understanding of her-self from all sexual relationships with men, past and pres-ent, including the lover who became her second husband, she has learned that "everyone ends up moving alone towards the self." Having sold the house she lived in with her two husbands, she is now occupying the annex of a house belonging to a dignified older black colleague and political ally, Zeph Rapulana. With him, for the first time in her life she was "involved in the being of a man to whom she knew no sexual pull." It is for her a deep, satisfying friendship, in which, through their shared work and understanding, Vera feels that "they belonged together as a single sex, a reconciliation of all each had experienced, he as a man, she as a woman."

Then, in an enigmatic ending, taking up less than a full page of print, Vera has a middle-of-the-night encounter in Zeph's house that is as startling to her as it is to the reader. She learns something about him that compels her to face a yet deeper aloneness. Afterward, she steps out into the garden, into "the biting ebony-blue of winter air as if she dived into the delicious shock of it . . . everything stripped. Not a leaf on the scoured smooth limbs of the trees . . . dried palm fronds still as her fingers. . . . A thick trail of smashed ice crackling light, stars blinded her as she let her head dip back; under the swing of the sky she stood, feet planted, on the axis of the night world"—alone, at the center of the labyrinth. "Vera walked there, for a while. And then"—the last sentence in the book—"took up her way, breath scrolling out, a signature before her." She leaves the center of the labyrinth. "None to accompany me on this path: / Nightfall"—not "in Autumn" but . . . in winter. The cold hard truth. Stark, yes, but strangely exhilarating, for Vera and for us.

It is exhilarating for us precisely because the truth of fine fiction like Gordimer's is the truth of human life. As we follow Vera in her path to intimacy with herself, Gordimer both discloses us to ourselves and shows us the ways we resist that disclosure. She heightens our awareness of the preciousness of what is won and of the elusiveness of the goal—of how limited our consciousness of ourselves is, even when, like Vera, we think we have reached the end of our inner journey. So that—but only at the last page of the book—we, with her, understand better the meaning of its first epigraph: "We must never be afraid to go too far, for truth lies beyond" (Marcel Proust).

Is it true, as Gordimer says, that "everyone ends up moving alone towards the self"? I do not know; I suspect that in some sense it is. I know that this is my truth, and not just in the physical sense of living alone. I have always understood that as a nun vowed to celibacy, I was renouncing conjugal love. But I have learned only over a long period of time that the vow is not merely a promise I made once, intending not to break it in some sexual way. It is an ongoing process, requiring an ever deeper and unselfish chastity of the heart, of the affections. And for me—though perhaps not for others—a deeper human aloneness than I had imagined. Just as, I reckon, any long-enduring marriage asks more of the spouses than they had dreamed of in the first heady years of romantic love.

I learned this chiefly from falling in love several times, once seriously, from undergoing that sweet, potent, preoccupying emotion that makes the world a wonderful place to be in, and oneself and the beloved the most fascinating people in it. I am certainly not going to try to explain this inexplicable phenomenon, rising somewhere from the depths of the unconscious, making us slightly, but oh so happily, mad. Thomas Mann was wise to say in *The Magic Mountain:* "Love is always simply itself, both as a subtle affirmation of life and as the highest passion; love is our sympathy with organic life, the touchingly lustful embrace of what is destined to decay. . . . In God's good name, leave the meaning of love unresolved." He is right; leave the meaning of love alone. And the feeling of falling in love, wondrous as it is, is itself "destined to decay"; it cannot last. The real love that may or may not follow upon it requires the down and dirty business of growing in self-sacrificing acceptance of the otherness of the one who stands before us, perhaps quite unlike that fantastic person who captivated the equally fantastic person we were while under its spell.

Because of my commitment to celibacy and the commitment of the one I loved, the sacrifice exacted in order to be true to those commitments—true to our selves—meant "to have and have not," the cost of real love being the renunciation even of presence to each other. So I know something of the longing for the kind of intimacy that falling in love brings with it, the desire to know everything about the beloved, to share oneself completely. And of what Virginia Woolf means by comparing reading to the act of love.

And what of intimacy with God? What can we say about this in a spirituality of reading, the search for the true self, for the God within, as it may be pursued in reading? Now we can go more deeply into the matter than noting the similarities of silence, physical stillness, and focused attention that reading and meditation share. We might, following the clues that reading gives us, think of meditation as an opportunity to reflect on our conversation with ourselves in the "presence" of another, as we may do when we read. We might imagine God overhearing us, "reading" us as we really are, good and bad, our naked selves. That already feels more intimate to me than the traditional definition of prayer as the "lifting up of the mind and heart to God," which, for me at least, seems to call for getting all dressed up in my Sunday best as I am likely to do in more formal prayer.

But since intimacy, an exchange of selves, must be reciprocal to be genuine, to seek it in prayer is to understand that we have been invited to be present at God's conversation with God's self, to overhear God's own thoughts and concerns and hopes for us, for others, for the world, invited into God's interiority. All of this gives the phrase "union with God in prayer," a phrase I've heard and used myself for years with only the vaguest appreciation of the intimate charge that it carries, another valence. It seems to mean that my spiritual story cannot be just about "God and me." God's story is surely bigger than that.

Gordimer's Vera, who is an atheist, would find this talk of intimacy with God incomprehensible, I am sure. Yet I am more like her than she might imagine, than I might have thought myself. Here is an entry from my journal for January 1998. In a kind of summary of the previous five or six years, after noting an ongoing experience of Jesus, the Lamb of God, within me, as me, bearing, absorbing, taking away my sin, my shame, my pain, I wrote, "And an almost subconscious sense of—'Well, even if he doesn't exist, it's worthwhile because I'm finding myself.'" Even if he doesn't exist! Much later, realizing how faithless that was, I began to pray the apparently contradictory but honest prayer, "Lord, I believe, help my unbelief" (Mark 9:23). I was—am—passing, still and slowly, from the kind of belief that merely gives lip service to Catholic dogma, or finds it intellectually engaging, to a faith that sees, however dimly, the meaning of these basic Christian doctrines for my life.

And like Vera, I know that "truth lies beyond." I know that faith—like chastity, like intimacy, like the journey to the self—is an ongoing process. Yes, we do walk the labyrinth to the center of ever greater knowledge of ourselves as we do in books like Gordimer's. We may also learn from them, as Vera learned, that no single human relationship can fulfill us, draw a small circle around who we are or can be. Others, alas, are as limited, as frail—and as mortal—as we are. We will be compelled, somehow, to leave the center we have found, and continue on our journey. For, self-transcending beings that we are, it is not the center that symbolizes our true selves but the entire labyrinth. If we are courageous enough not to give up on life, on human relationships, or on ourselves—as we surmise from the tone of the last passage is the case with Vera—we will walk it many times, inward and outward, each time going more deeply within, each time reaching out in a wider embrace. And we will have, thanks to the writers among us, not a single book—no single book can satisfy us, either—but many books to accompany us like intimate friends at each stage of the journey, to lead us yet closer to the truth that, as long as we live, lies beyond.

Unlike Vera, in the doctrines and dogmas of my faith, to which I could cling even in my unbelief, I have always had at least a small hope, sometimes a blind trust, and finally in these later years, even a quiet confidence that I am not alone on my journey. God doesn't wait for us to reach the goal; God is with us at every step. Like the mysterious stranger with whom Jacob wrestles in the book of Genesis (32:24–30), or who meets the disciples on the road to Emmaus (Luke 24:13–32), God blesses us on the way, is the companion who breaks bread with us, even when we, like them, don't recognize him.

Reflection
POETRY:
A DEEPER INTIMACY

Lyric poetry, it seems to me, is the most intimate of the imaginative literary genres. Where each word, phrase, and sentence is weighed for its sound and rhythm, weighted with meaning and emotion, we are invited to share, in a persona created by the author, the speaker's experience—a particular feeling, a perception, a mood, an insight into life or nature. Just last night on public TV, I heard 2002 Pulitzer Prize winner Carl Dennis, speaking as a writer of lyric poetry, say that he writes his poems as one person to another, like writing to an "unknown friend." The poem is offered to us in a highly crafted form, to be sure, but as if still hot from the anvil of both the original experience and the writing of the poem itself. In a good poem immediacy and intimacy are forged together.

At the same time, in its very craftedness, it asks more of us and yields, in proportion to its length, more than other forms of literature. If in silent reading in general, as Alberto Manguel says, in *The History of Reading*, we are free "to pause, to inspect words at leisure, drawing new notions from them, allowing comparison from memory," then in lyric poetry we are compelled in several different ways to unhurriedness and introspection. While the line of print in a novel, for instance, proceeds mostly in unbroken fashion from one margin of the page to the other, and plot and character development drive us forward until we reach a sense of wholeness at its end, to read a poem well we must go slowly, attend more carefully to all its elements. Line breaks and their meaning arrest us. Our innate sense of rhythm and, in some poems, our appetite for rhyme, though less robust in us than in readers of the past, are fully satisfied. Above all, we must savor the words themselves for their full import, their sound and resonances, their relationship to other words in the line, the poem. A short poem, like some novels, may ask big questions, but it delivers its answers, its wholeness, in images that are at once concrete and universal—"a world in a grain of sand," as William Blake said.

In the image of an intimate supper, "Love III," by George Herbert, encompasses themes no less grand than sin and redemption, exquisitely capturing the delicate courtesy of its host:

> Love bade me welcome, yet my soul drew back,
>   Guilty of dust and sin.
> But quick-eyed Love, observing me grow slack
>   From my first entrance in,
> Drew nearer to me, sweetly questioning
>   If I lacked anything.
>
> "A guest," I answered," worthy to be here."
>   Love said, "You shall be he."
> "I, the unkind, ungrateful? Ah, my dear,
>   I cannot look on thee."
> Love took my hand and smiling did reply,
>   "Who made the eyes but I?"
>
> "Truth, Lord, but I have marred them;
>   let my shame

Go where it doth deserve."
"And know you not," says Love,
    "who bore the blame?"
"My dear, then I will serve."
"You must sit down," says Love,
    "and taste my meat."
So I did sit and eat.

While I find in the poem a poignantly tender portrayal of redemption, it's odd, perhaps, that it is not a "holy" thought from it that has stayed with me. It is the phrase "quick-eyed Love." Those three words hold for me all the keen attentiveness of lovers to each other, eager to know and meet every desire of the beloved. And although I am not, to my loss and regret, a great reader of poetry, with the exception of passages of prose from the Bible, over the years I have gathered into myself more phrases and lines of poetry than of any other genre; they have become part of me. Like small jewels in my own literary labyrinth, they crystallize and reflect experiences I have had, and mark the path that I have taken.

In e. e. cummings's "in Just-," "and bettyandisabel come dancing / from hop-scotch and jump-rope and / it's / spring..." And there, in my mind's eye, are bobbyann-andi, arms entwined, inseparable five-year-old friends.

Billy Collins brings me back to my "First Reader": "I can see them standing politely on the wide pages / that I was still learning to turn, / Jane in a blue jumper, Dick with his crayon brown hair, / . . . and he and she / are always pointing at something and shouting 'Look!'" (They were!)

John Donne's "Batter my heart, Three-Personed God . . . for I / Except You enthrall me, never shall be free / Nor ever chaste, except You ravish me" mirrors me to myself as I have struggled to remain faithful to the vow of celibacy. And in Gerard Manley Hopkins's "I wake and feel the fell of dark, not day," when "I am gall, I am heartburn. God's most deep decree / Bitter would have me taste; my taste was me," I am reminded of the acrid self-disgust I experienced as an active alcoholic.

"After great pain, a formal feeling comes— / the Nerves sit ceremonious like Tombs," says Emily Dickinson, expressing the strange stunned sensation of feeling nothing that may follow grief, as it did for me when my parents died. And I see now why Yeats's "Sailing to Byzantium" impressed itself upon me years ago, in anticipation of growing older, the body failing, the mind, the soul, unregarded by others: "That is no country for old men. The young / In one another's arms, birds in the

trees / ... The salmon-falls, the mackerel-crowded seas. ...
Caught in that sensual music all neglect / Monuments of
unageing intellect. / An aged man is but a paltry thing, /
A tattered coat upon a stick, unless / Soul clap its hands
and sing, and louder sing."

And then there are the phrases inexplicably remembered: "Nine bean-rows will I have there"—from Yeats
again, "The Lake Isle of Innisfree"—because it expresses
some simple perfection? Or from Joseph Brodsky's "Flight
into Egypt" (translated from the Russian by Seamus
Heaney), an utterly unromanticized rendering of Jesus,
Mary, and Joseph huddled in the cave amid "the fug of
fodder and old clothes. / ... That night, as three, they
were at peace. / Smoke like a shy retiring guest / Slipped
out the door. There was one far-off / Heavy sigh from the
mule. Or the ox." I cherish those last three words, and I
can't tell you why.

Lyric poetry, too, when shared, can reach beyond ourselves and the poet to others in an especially intimate way.
I loved the PBS project in which ordinary people—those I
remember, a vibrant nine- or ten-year-old girl, a dread-
locked jazz musician in Chicago, a construction worker
from Massachusetts—recited a poem for us, and told us
why it was their favorite. The variety of people and their

choices was rich, the experience more personal and touching than hearing former poet laureate Robert Pinsky read
a poem for us, as he often did (for me, even more touching
than hearing a poet read her own work). The construction
worker selected several stanzas of Walt Whitman's "Song
of Myself," and we, listening to him recite and talk about
it, enjoyed a brief but intimately revealing moment not
only with Walt but with him.

A poem can also bespeak the sentiment of a nation.
The Internet was alive after September 11 with people
drawn together to remind one another of W. H. Auden's
"September 1, 1939." (You must read the whole poem, if
you haven't already done so.) "The unmentionable odour
of death / Offends the September night. / . . . Into this
neutral air / Where blind skyscrapers use / Their full
height to proclaim / The strength of Collective Man /
Each language pours its vain / Competitive excuse: / But
who can live for long / In an euphoric dream." And, in
counterpoint to the lines that read, "For the error bred in
the bone / Of each woman and each man / Craves what it
cannot have, / Not universal love / But to be loved alone,"
the conclusion of the penultimate stanza: "We must love
one another or die."

Over the years of my life as a nun, I have recited and

chanted, silently read and meditated on the poems in the Bible—the canticles of Moses, Miriam, the somber and stately cadences of the Suffering Servant Song in Isaiah 53, the Psalms, the Song of Solomon, Mary's "Magnificat," Simeon's canticle. But I have considered them more as prayer than as poetry. (Some of them, especially some of the psalms, are explicit prayers, spoken directly to God.) By now, like long-fingered coins well worn from use, they have lost the sharpness of their imprint for me, and I some-times read them lickety-split, hardly pausing to think, let alone pray. I might do well to revisit them as the poetry that they are, pausing to note, as I would in reading a poem, the human emotions of fear, anger, sorrow, re-pentance, hope, joy, love, praise, and thanksgiving that they express; to plumb the images of God as warrior, king, bridegroom, shepherd, eagle, rock, lamp; myself as a drowning man, or a senseless mule, my heart melting like wax, my soul thirsting for God.

And I haven't thought to look to "secular" poetry, even when its themes are religious, as texts for meditation. I asked one of my nun friends, Ellie, who I know loves po-etry, whether she uses it in private prayer. She does, and said that she sometimes reads it aloud, a practice, as we saw earlier, that is recommended in the method of reading /

prayer known as *lectio divina*. She attested to the shift of consciousness the poems invite, the focus they provide, the striking beauty of their language. Poetry doesn't always put her in conscious contact with God, but even in poems like those of Mary Oliver, many about nature, beneath the surface of the poem—"the implicate level," as Oliver calls it—she finds matter for meditation on the mysteries of life, death, choice. Ellie's community also uses secular poetry at times in their shared prayer. The day that we spoke about this, two days before Christmas, she had chosen Denise Levertov's "Annunciation" as the text for their morning prayer. She read it out loud, and after a period for silent reflection, each spoke to God the prayers of petition suggested to her by the poem.

Now I think that my prayer life would also be re-freshed if I were to look to secular poetry—Oliver, Lever-tov, Auden—as matter for meditation. Using the Ignatian method of prayer I learned in the novitiate, I should read Herbert's "Love III," for instance, as a kind of scripture, imagine myself (like Herbert when writing the poem?) as the guest, "guilty of dust and sin," imagine Love "sweetly questioning me," my answers, Love "taking my hand." That would be entering into the intimacy and immediacy of the poem more completely than I have ever done, when, however much I've appreciated Herbert's imagery, I remained an onlooker to the intimacy of others, an "overhearer" of their conversation. And I might then come myself to a yet deeper intimacy with the host, break bread with Love, *recognized* this time in a poem become prayer for me.

OUR BODIES, OUR SELVES

The Erotic in Spirituality and in Literature

THE CENTER of the labyrinth is often called the rosette. It is made up of a six-petaled rose-shaped area," says Lauren Artress in *Walking a Sacred Path: Rediscovering the Labyrinth as a Spiritual Tool*, the rose symbolizing, among other realities, both passionate human love and divine love. The other day, I snitched a few roses from the huge bush growing almost to the second-floor porch of the house next door. I have them on my bookcase now, the most beautiful creamy white, opening out to a translucent pearly pink as the buds unfold. They literally stop me in my tracks when my eyes fall on them. Roses, with their layered loveliness, speak to me of the self in its unfolding—and of female sexuality. Of body and soul—our whole selves—embraced in one symbol. It is when body and soul meet in the portrayal of sex in literature that I find the genuinely erotic. And I think the erotic, and erotic literature, should have a place in our spirituality.

"Let him kiss me with the kisses of his mouth." This is the first line of the Song of Solomon, also known as the Song of Songs or the Canticle of Canticles, a collection of disjointed love songs found in the Bible, whose provenance and authorship remain a mystery to scholars even today. I vividly remember my first encounter with this text. I had already decided to enter the convent and was attending daily mass while at home during the summer of my junior year in college. Before the reform of the liturgical calendar after Vatican II, July 2 marked the Feast of the Visitation. The Gospel of the day tells us that Mary, carrying Jesus in her womb, "set out and went with haste to a Judean town in the hill country" (Luke 1:39) to visit her cousin Elizabeth. And in that marvelous way the medieval church had of linking texts by (sometimes fanciful or tenuous) association, the first reading for the feast was taken from the second chapter of the Canticle. "Look, he comes, / leaping upon the mountains, / bounding over the hills. . . . My beloved speaks and says to me: / 'Arise, my love, my fair one, and come away; / for now the winter is past, /

the rain is over and gone. / The flowers appear on the earth; / the time of singing has come, / and the voice of the turtledove / is heard in our land.'" I found the text beautifully sensuous; it gave me my first glimpse of the mysticism of Catherine of Siena, Bernard of Clairvaux, John of the Cross, Teresa of Ávila, in whose writings the experience of erotic love provides the imagery for the love between God and the soul. And the Canticle gave me, from scripture itself, a spiritual place to put my own burgeoning erotic desires.

"The problem with the Song of Songs," says James A. Fischer, C.M., in *The Collegeville Bible Commentary*, "is to find some reason why it should be in the Bible . . . it does not even mention God." But there it was, and later, both Jews and Christians allegorized it to stand for the marriage of God and the chosen people, or of Christ and the church, or, as in the mystics, the union of the soul and God. After commenting on the tendency to give the Song a symbolic meaning and thus avoid the plain references to physical love and its ecstatic emotions, Fischer concludes:

> Completely different is the wisdom interpretation. In this view the Song is indeed composed of popular love songs joined only by a whisper of a plot. Human love is good. It need not be justified by es-

oteric spiritual reasonings. The sages taught that
God's order and goodness pervade all; there is no
such thing as the secular. The love of a boy and a
girl is one of God's beauties.

Yes, our bodies, our selves, including our sexuality, are
shot through with the spirit of God—God "breathed into
his nostrils the breath [spirit] of life and the man became a
living being" (Genesis 2:7). Of all earthly realities, more
than bread and wine and oils and incense, human beings,
body and soul, are sacraments of God, of God's presence:
"in the image of God he created them; male and female he
created them. . . . And God saw everything he had made,
and indeed it was very good" (Genesis 1:27, 31). Granted,
the Genesis account describes human nature before the
fall, but unlike some forms of Protestantism, Catholicism
has always maintained the *essential* goodness of nature,
that we are not, even in our fallen and sinful state, evil by
nature. And if we are believers in the incarnation, that
nature—all of it—has been redeemed and sanctified by
the Christ and the indwelling Spirit.

Sister Wendy, the British nun whose lectures on art
have captivated viewers of public TV, disarmingly expresses this view in her comments on Michelangelo's Adam,

sprawling "in his naked male beauty" on the ceiling of the
Sistine Chapel, and on the "lovely and fluffy pubic hair" in
a nude by Stanley Spencer, thus confounding the press and
interviewer Bill Moyers. She stands firmly in that older
Christian pre-puritancial, pre-Jansenistic (pre–fig leaf!)
tradition that affirms the natural beauty and goodness of
the human body. So I'm with Wendy. And I think it just
right that the Song of Songs should have a place in our
scriptures—and just as it is, without overlaying it with all
kinds of allegorical, disembodied interpretations.

When I was a teenager, the nuns told us that our bodies were "temples of the Holy Ghost," thus obliquely cau-
tioning us not to defile them in sexual exploration. The
expression meant nothing to us; we took it almost as a joke.
Had I been told, however, that my body was myself, as
much a part of me as my most secret thoughts, it might
have meant more. I tried to get this notion across to my
sophomore girls at The Ursuline School in a course on
sexuality that I initiated. (I recall the first time I used the
word *penis* in class. To tell the truth, I had not used it very
many times before that moment.) They would not want,
would they, I asked, other people reading their mail, or
their diaries. Why, then, thoughtlessly or indiscriminately
share this part of themselves? I tried, too, to get them to see

that boys were people, with their own thoughts and feelings—were selves, as I would put it now. That was the
harder task, and I don't think I succeeded at all.

I am concerned here to reclaim the erotic for spirituality and to reclaim the part that the erotic in literature may
play in our spirituality. The matter is complex, subtle; I
only offer the guidelines that work for me. For me, it is not
what a piece of literature portrays but the characteristics
of the portrayal that provide the discriminating criteria
between the erotic and its stunting counterfeits: the pornographic, the lewd, the artistically spurious. It is the presence of spirit in a description of the depths of human
passion, and yes, pleasure, that makes a difference. It is the
meaning of the sexual act (a "soul" question) for the characters involved, and in the story that is being told. Is the
portrayal of sex integral to the work? Is the portrayal of
other feelings—of grief, anger, jealousy, joy—of the same
intensity as that of the portrayal of sex? Is it consonant
with the emotional timbre of the work as a whole?

Language and style, too, have a role in the erotic. I am
thinking of erotic passages in Updike, for instance, that
rise to the level of the lyrical. He has been criticized by
some for excesses of language and sentiment in general.
But his lyricism works for me, because it is not merely or-
namental, laid like a lacquer on top of whatever he is de-

scribing. Rather, for me, his metaphoric language reaches into and grows out of the reality he is describing. Which is not to say that only the lyrical can be erotic. Gordimer's descriptions of sex can be brief, sometimes blunt in their physicality. They are powerful, unromantic, in books that deal with issues that are anything but romantic. So the aesthetic value of appropriateness comes into play as well.

Then there are the intentions of the writer—and of the reader. Without the dimension of depth, emotional integration with the whole work, and language faithful to what is being described, we are left with the cartoon characters of bodice rippers who engage in best-seller sex not because it arises out of the exigencies of plot or character but because it has been twenty-five pages since the last sex scene. It is injected by the author to attract and hold the attention of readers who, even if they do not skip through the book looking for "the good parts," as many of us did as adolescents, need a little sex thown in now and then to keep them going. Or worse, in my opinion, we are seduced by the (often quite graphic) sex scenes in some of the better-written romances, which, precisely because of their literary pretensions and subtler characterization, claim to offer something more than sex. Maybe they do, but the presentation of sex—about every twenty-five pages—does not ring true for me, and it vitiates whatever other merits the work might have. It feels like cheap sex and spurious art to me, the spiritual equivalent of junk food; it may look like an éclair, but it's really a Twinkie.

Pornographic literature depicts sex in explicit or bizarre or even intentionally degrading and dehumanizing detail. Designed by the author and used by the reader specifically for sexual stimulation, it serves no literary end. It commodifies sex. It is a product, not literature, and the person who uses it is primarily a consumer, not a reader. In its baser forms the pornographic appeals to the baser instincts, the selfish, the violent in us. In its milder forms, pornography presents the physical/sexual to appeal only to the physical/sexual in us, and hence tells less than half the story of being human. And we are left with a world in which, contrary to a spirituality that finds God in all things, including sex, nothing is sacred, everything is profane.

In an odd way, the Roman Catholic Church itself has conspired with the culture to reduce the meaning of sexuality to the purely physical. In its official position, the church has long adhered to a rigid natural-law biologism that sees every sexual act as ordered to procreation, and hence permitted only in marriage. While the 1969 encyclical *Humanae vitae* did acknowledge that intercourse may express the mutual love of the spouses (most couples had figured this out on their own), it condemned the use of ar-

tificial birth control as contrary to nature. Such a view, instead of acknowledging and accepting sexuality as part of
being human, and expressive of a range of human emotions, desires, and intentions, reduces it and its place in our
spirituality to a gritting-of-the-teeth morality, in which, outside of marriage—and even sometimes within it (during
fertile periods for those not wishing to conceive)—every
natural sexual thought, feeling, and impulse is a tempta-
tion to be resisted, or an "occasion of sin" (something that
might predispose or move us to a sinful act). "One thing
leads to another," as we were warned growing up.

Because of this kind of instruction, there were longer
lines outside the confessionals of those priests who were
known in the old days to be more lenient in giving abso-
lution for sins like impure thoughts, petting, masturbation,
the use of artificial birth control, and so on. Today, few of
the parish priests or spiritual advisers or counselors that I
know would attempt to inculcate or enforce the church's
official position on sex. Its inflexibility and narrowness have
made it largely irrelevant, especially in our highly sexualized culture, and especially—and sadly—among adolescents, who most need a sound, healthy, genuine spirituality
of sex.

Both the culture and the church have further diminished sexuality and the erotic by overgenitalizing them.

When I decided to become a nun, my limited sexual experience and the experience of my own body had given me some sense of what the renunciation of genital sexual expression entailed. Of course, I and other women who were contemplating religious life also thought deeply about not having families of our own. But it was only in my forties, when I experienced in myself the ticking of the famous biological clock that would make bearing children impossible for me, that I came to another experience and another meaning in my vow of celibacy. As I wrote in a 1981 article in *America* entitled "A New Word on Celibacy," it is not only vagina but womb and breasts that long with a biological urgency for expression.

In the wake of the oceans of ink spilled on celibacy in Catholic circles during the sixties and seventies, I dared to give the article that title because none of the material I was familiar with had ever dealt with this aspect of the topic. I found the omission strange; since the procreation of children is of such prime importance in the teaching of the church on sex one would have thought that a key consideration in the renunciation of marriage in celibacy would be the renunciation of the right to have children. Not nearly so surprising to us now as it was in 1981 was my conclusion that this had been the case because the terms of the public theological/spiritual discussion about celibacy have been set by men, determined by the experience of men, and have neglected and ignored an enormously important aspect of the sexuality of women.

As a woman, I cannot imagine that nursing a baby, for instance, is not at times a profoundly sexual and spiritual—hence, erotic—experience, body and soul engaged as one in so intimate an act. Save for the poem from which the title of *Let Us Now Praise Famous Men* is taken, James Agee concludes his book with a long, meticulously sensuous, beautifully spiritual, erotic description of a mother and her baby. I give only a brief excerpt:

> He is nursing. His hands are blundering at her breast blindly, as if themselves each were a new born creature, or as if they were sobbing, ecstatic with love; his mouth is intensely absorbed at her nipple as if in rapid kisses, with small and swift sounds of moisture; his eyes are squeezed shut; and now, for breath, he draws away, and lets out a sharp, short, whispered ahh, the hands and his eyelids relaxing, and immediately resumes; and all the while, his face is beatific, the face of one at rest in paradise, and in all this her gentle and sober, earnest face is not altered out of its deep slantwise gazing . . . and I see how against her body he is so many things in

one, the child in the melodies of the womb, the Madonna's son, human divinity sunken from the cross at rest against his mother.

Yet we shun thinking or speaking about matters like this as erotic, let alone as spiritual. The problem is not in the act or in naming it erotic. It is in our reducing the meaning and intention of genuinely erotic actions so exclusively to genital expression, certainly out of place in our dealings with children. I am reminded again of Granny Maraffi. To my adolescent embarrassment, she sometimes, always with a sweet smile, softly touched the small breasts growing beneath my dress. She was, I imagine now, remembering and anticipating for me as I grew into womanhood the natural, beautiful, sacred, erotic experience of nursing a baby.

Of course, the church and other guardians of public morality have a point. Sex is powerful; passionate love can be transgressive of the good order of society. It can be sinful, causing great harm and pain to others. And the erotic in literature may beguile, seduce. The last is one of the reasons that we as young nuns were not permitted to read or even to study novels. The solution is not, however, to deny but to recognize and accept the power of this aspect of our humanity, and to channel it into fruitfulness and productivity, to see it as a gift from God, to find God in it. And to rejoice in being fully alive, body and soul, for the glory of God. "The glory of God is the human being fully alive," as St. Irenaeus said.

For me as a celibate, a virgin, not a mother, reading has played an important—I would say a necessary—part in my coming to know what a great human good I renounced when I took the vow of chastity over forty-five years ago. I have come to acknowledge the immense power of sexuality, for good or for ill, and to feel compassion for those illicitly under its sway. I see sex as able in a profound way to express the self, to give that self in love, and hence become a vessel of intimacy with another. Reading has helped me to imagine the "joy of sex" (no, I have not read the book), the intensity of its pleasure, the solace it can offer, the sometimes tragic—and sometimes comic—aspects of it. Giving all of that up has been costly. On the other hand, especially as I grow older, I have learned from life and from literature how difficult it is for two people to live faithfully together for a lifetime; I marvel that any marriage succeeds. I know, too, that children can be the cause of the deepest pain as well as the deepest happiness. And at times I believe that I have been spared perhaps more than I have sacrificed.

But whatever the story of our lives, I believe that our

spirituality, our search for the true self, must encompass our bodies. How, then, could a spirituality of reading eschew the erotic, where body and soul embrace? As Rabbi Akiba said, "If all the books of the Bible are holy, then the Song of Songs is the Holy of Holies."

A LITERARY
CONTEMPLATIO AD AMOREM

Imagination: Faith, Hope, and Love

NIEBUHR STARTLED ME one day in class by saying that perception is a matter of choice, that we do not, as I had thoughtlessly assumed, merely see what is there to be seen, objects reflecting light to our eyeballs. We *choose* what to see and how to see it. Reading has compelled me to focus my vision. When I read a fine description of a familiar scene from nature, for instance, I experience a complex delight. Yes, I say, that's it. That's what I have seen. But the description does more than that. It articulates, clarifies, illumines my vision, making me see better than I have before the fierce and fragile beauty of the world.

And reading has changed how I see, or have not seen, others (isn't this the point of Ralph Ellison's *Invisible Man*?); it enlarges my vision. Alice Walker's *The Color Purple* makes me see the world through the eyes of a black woman. In Saul Bellow's *Mr. Sammler's Planet*, I live inside the head of a Jewish intellectual in Chicago. I become intimate with a reluctant Czech dissident in Milan Kundera's *The Unbearable Lightness of Being*. I can hardly conceive how limited my perception would be without the books I have been privileged to read, how superficial my understanding of others, how undeveloped my sympathies. And I mean here, especially, without fiction, which puts flesh and blood on, and soul and feeling in, other human beings. Precisely because of its appeal to my imagination, which *Webster's* dictionary defines as "the act or power of forming a mental image of something not present to the senses or never before wholly perceived in reality," in fiction I come to know and understand people I may not have met otherwise. And thus I am persuaded to a more compassionate, generous, and loving response in my life beyond books.

Jesus knew this. What are his parables but stories, inviting and, if we heed them, compelling us to *imagine* things as other than we had thought? God as a prodigally loving father rather than a punishing judge. The reign of God as a place where power, status, and wealth count for nothing, but where "the last"—prostitutes, tax collectors, sinners—"will be first" (Mark 10:31). What was it that made the difference in the priest, the Levite, and the Samaritan (Luke 10:30ff), all encountering the man who fell among robbers and was left for dead? It was not the law that was effective here; the priest and the Levite, who knew the law, shunned the apparently dead man out of fear of defilement. No, it was a lively moral imagination, the ability of the Samaritan to imagine himself in the victim's place, imagine his pain and need as his own, and imagine himself as called, and able, to remedy his neighbor's plight. And it is to the imaginations of hearers/readers of the parable that Jesus appeals. Doesn't the story in its simple clarity bring us to pass judgment on the priest and the Levite, only to compel us to recognize and acknowledge their presence in ourselves, law-abiding—and coldhearted—as we are? And can we imagine ourselves as we could be if we saw our fellows, as the Samaritan did, with "the eye of love," with faith?

So much is made of the debate between faith and reason, between faith and science, faith and philosophy. And we neglect, I fear, the part that the imagination—something of a stepdaughter in the house of the intellect—may play in our faith, not only in our moral lives, as above, but in our prayer, worship, and beliefs. St. Ignatius, for one, understood how the imagination, far from arguing with faith, may nourish it in prayer. The second prelude to contemplation as outlined in his Spiritual Exercises is devoted to the imagination. In contemplating the Nativity, for example, the saint counsels us to see "in imagination the way from Nazareth to Bethlehem. Consider its length, its breadth; whether level, or through valleys and over hills. Observe also the place or cave where Christ is born; whether big or little; whether high or low; and how it is arranged." In the exercise known as the application of the senses—a method of private prayer that can be used in contemplating any scene from the Bible—we are to see the persons, hear what they are saying, to embrace and kiss the place where the persons stand or are seated, to "smell the infinite fragrance and taste the infinite sweetness of the divinity."

Our imaginations have their place in our beliefs as well. I am often disconcerted by the way Catholics recite the Nicene Creed at the Sunday liturgy. We, including me, rush through it, our voices devoid of inflection, as if it were a list of the facts that we have to know and believe to certify as bona fide members of the church. "We believe in one God . . . maker of heaven and earth. . . . We believe in one Lord, Jesus Christ, the only Son of God, eternally begotten of the Father, God from God, Light from Light." But one day, my attention was arrested by that phrase "Light from Light." This is not a fact; I knew that God cannot be *defined* as light. It is an image for an aspect of God, as is the ancient hallowed name of Father, both attempts of our limited language and our finite minds—our imaginations—to express what is essentially ineffable, the divine.

Just so, we use images to express the boundlessness of human hope and desire—for eternal life, unconditional love, unlimited communion, as Catholics do when they profess belief in "the communion of saints, the forgiveness of sins, the resurrection of the body, and life everlasting" in the Apostles' Creed. None of these articles of faith, including those that recall the story of Jesus, are provable in the way of mathematics or science. Or even of history. It is central to my own belief that Jesus was a real historical person; historical study can support my belief but it cannot prove it. The truths of faith are precisely, according to traditional Roman Catholic teaching, those that cannot be known by reason alone; that is why they are "revealed."

But they *are* true in speaking to our deepest longings: "Faith is the assurance of things hoped for [faith and hope mixed together], the conviction of things not seen," as the Letter to the Hebrews 11:1 puts it. They are true as the best

poetry is true. They give us a way of making real to ourselves "something not present to the senses, or never before wholly perceived in reality." We have no other way,
really. As C. S. Lewis said to Tolkien, the latter's "reluc-
tance to understand [the mysteries of faith] comes from a
failure of the imagination." Whatever our beliefs, it is often a lack of imagination as much as a lack of faith—or
hope, or love—that we suffer from. So I think we would
do well to savor the words of our prayers as if they were
poetry. And let our imaginations feed upon the images
they present so that we may believe just a little that "no eye
has seen, nor ear heard, nor the human heart conceived,
what God has prepared for those who love Him" (1 Corinthians 2:9).

Thus, in this spirituality of reading, I want to commem-
orate those who have nourished, challenged, stretched our
imaginations in so many ways, who have helped us to believe, and hope, and love. I want to express my belief in
another "communion of saints"—a *communio sanctorum*—
another community of people transcending the bounds of
time and space, who, as canonized and uncanonized saints
are for Roman Catholics, are our patrons, our friends, our
companions on the journey. As the Epistle to the Hebrews
says of Abraham, Moses, Rahab, David, and others, we

readers "have so great a cloud of witnesses" (11:29–12:1) in our great writers. They have finely observed and given testimony to the mysteries of life and personality, to motive, intention, and action, to passion and suffering and death, to love and hatred, to hope and fear, to evil, to bliss, to the beauty of nature and our powerlessness under its ravages, to our struggle with human movements and institutions, to our search for meaning and the good, and some of them, explicitly, to our search for God.

Start wherever you will: With Homer's Achilles, the great hero, sulking in his tent like a big spoiled child. Or with Abraham as he holds the sacrificial knife over his son Isaac in obedience to God's command. Or with Dante's Paolo and Francesca, illicit lovers reading a book together in a quiet garden: "They read no more that day" (an exquisite example of understated eroticism). Skip a few centuries to Dorothea Brooke, a woman with a passionate idealistic nature, "a later-born Teresa" of Ávila, who longs to do great and good deeds, only to become "foundress of nothing," as George Eliot introduces her in the Prelude to *Middlemarch*.

Come closer to our own times. Learn the emotional geography of Faulkner's Yoknapatawpha County. Visit a magically real South American country with Gabriel Gar-

cía Márquez. In the fine biographies that rise to the level of
art themselves, enter the mind, heart, soul, and body of
David McCullough's John Adams, the prickly, learned, independent son of a Yankee farmer who became the second
president of the United States—in a great book about a
man whose greatness has been underestimated until now;
read the honest, ever-so-faithful correspondence between
him and the wise and valiant Abigail, his wife, a moving
love story in itself, and a treasury of a kind of formal yet
intimate language largely lost to us. And in the "authors"
of authors—Leon Edel's Henry James, Richard Ellmann's
James Joyce, Hermione Lee's Virginia Woolf—come to
know and appreciate, as best we can, the inner workings of
the creative life, its costs and its rewards.

Now, as if the outer circle of my imaginary labyrinth
were the globe itself, our inherited canon of mostly white
male Western authors has been enlarged to include other
voices, from other continents and cultures. When I read
Arundhati Roy's *The God of Small Things*, I had an opportunity to see India and its people from the viewpoint of a
native writer, a country different from the raj explored in
E. M. Forster's *Passage to India* or Paul Scott's *The Raj
Quartet*. There are few limits to what is available in literature to acquaint us, intimately, with one another, to enlarge
our understanding and sympathies, all the while giving us

keen pleasure. And I, for one, must confess that this canon has more profoundly influenced me in who I am, what I think and feel and do, than, with a few exceptions, the canonized saints of the Roman Catholic Church.

Further, I would have a literary/liturgical calendar that would mark an All Saints' Day (the church's omnium-gatherum feast) in which we celebrate those not registered in the established canons of great literature but lesser-known persons writing in, perhaps, less grand genres: the authors of short stories, mysteries, science fiction; nature writers, essayists, those who make us laugh—and our own particular favorites. I will not even try to be exhaustive. The point is that literature, like life, is not made up solely of great moments. Nor are we always up to reading the sublime. And I for one am thankful for all of those who have contributed to making my life as rich as it is.

More. In the term *communio sanctorum*, the genitive plural *sanctorum* can be read as both masculine and neuter, not only the community of holy people but of holy things. In her *Friends of God and Prophets: A Feminist Theological Reading of the Communion of Saints*, Elizabeth Johnson tells us that this meaning, more prevalent in the Eastern church than in the West, refers to those who share in the holy things, preeminently in the eucharist. You guessed it. My *communio sanctorum* would include books, and the worldwide community of readers from every age who have sat at the table of literature and partaken of the rich feast set before us. I am thinking not only of the eminent interpreters and critics who have influenced our understanding of what we read, but of all those who love reading.

I learn that the man who sells fresh fish on Thursdays and Fridays from the back of a van in New Rochelle sits in the front seat, between sales, reading. As he weighs and wraps my purchase, he cannot keep himself from telling me about his current book, John Steinbeck's *Tortilla Flats*. Martin, who cuts my hair in his kitchen, sprints over to his cluttered living room (he is also a dealer in collectibles) to show me the text he read in a course on world religions at NYU last semester. Good fish, a superb haircut—and *communio* in unexpected places, no?

And surely a desire for community accounts in some measure for the popularity of book clubs that we are witnessing today. I am thinking not so much of the small groups of people who have met for years to discuss books, or even of Oprah's book club, as of the growing national One Book movement. According to the Connecticut section of the Sunday, March 31, 2002, *New York Times,* the movement began on the West Coast when Nancy Pearl at the Washington Center for the Book, in Seattle, asked the question, "What if all Seattle read the same book?" It has spread to Chicago and New York, and to entire states, including Kentucky, Arkansas, and Rhode Island. New London, Connecticut, has initiated a regional program, reaching out to everyone in the area, from fourteen-year-olds to adults, with books available in all formats as well as in Spanish. And the organizers in Hartford passed over Mark Twain as their chosen author in favor of living writers who they hope will participate in the project. Writers, readers, adolescents, adults, people who speak different languages coming together to discuss a book.

Even more wide-reaching is the global BookCrossing book lovers' community that a friend of mine found on the Internet. To become a member you register on its site the title of a "book that speaks to you, that touches your life . . . that you want to share . . . with somone else," along with your journal comments about it. You then receive a BookCrossing ID number, making you a participant in a worldwide community of discussion about your book and others. Finally, you are to write BC's website address (http://www.bookcrossing.com) and your BCID inside the covers of favorite books you want to "release," and "give them away, or leave them where someone will find them." This, says the website, is "a fascinating exercise in fate, karma, or whatever you want to call the chain of events that can occur between two or more lives and one piece of literature." Or a fascinating exercise in "book providence" and "book kinship" rolled into one.

"What if?" asked the people in Seattle, no doubt intuiting in their question the wisdom in E. M. Forster's dictum "Only connect." At the very least, the remarkable growth of the book club phenomenon evidences both people's hunger for community in a fractured society, and the power of literature to bring them together in very personal ways. True, the conversation may enhance our understanding of a book or change our opinion about it. Beyond that, however, we reveal ourselves in conversations about books in ways that we wouldn't at a Tupperware party, for instance. And listening to others, we may also better understand ourselves, the people in our lives, our fellow readers, and even life itself—no small blessing.

My *communio sanctorum* would also include libraries, great and small, from the handsome cathedral-like Library of Congress to the four-room City Island library, where, through a computerized system, I can get any book held by the New York City branch libraries. And I would add bookstores, large and small, in which I always experience a sense of community with other browsing patrons. The atmosphere in the Yonkers Barnes & Noble, with its dark wooden bookshelves, the occasional comfortable chair, the attentive and helpful clerks, is not that of a bustling marketplace. Even with a gratifying number of people there, it is surprisingly quiet and reflective, and both the people and the place give me hope that there is a future for books in the electronic age.

None of this is to deny that those who never pick up a book can be good and can do, have done, great things. Nor do I deny that I have been influenced, hugely, by many other factors in my life, especially people. Or that there are bad books, shallow, sensational, deceitful, even evil books. But as Wayne Booth persuasively argues in *The Company We Keep*, "spending long hours in the company of the 'right' literary friends and avoiding 'bad (literary) company'" is a choice that we can make, and one with profound though subtle consequences for who we are.

I am not sure who first used the phrase "a community of memory and of hope," embracing both the past and the future. Books contain both our memories and our hopes, shape them, in some cases create them. Since the first human put chisel to stone, we have traveled a long distance in our inner and outward journeys, so much of what we know of those journeys preserved for us in writing. Now when an author puts the first word on paper or screen, she commits an act of hope. And every time we open a book, so do we. We hope for all kinds of things from a book—pleasure, knowledge, insight, intimacy, greater understanding of others and ourselves, beauty. But reading can also, in a deeper and more inchoate fashion, *give* us hope. Hope that there is a God whose extravagant fecundity is the source of the mysterious creative impulse of the artists among us. That the care and attention writers lavish on their characters are bestowed on us by our Creator. And that there is in life the kind of wholeness achieved in a great work of literature—a master narrative in which, though we cannot always see how, your story and mine have their part.

Now, as we move outward from the center to the circumference of this literary labyrinth, and then step back into the world, itself a tiny globe in a boundless universe, we may ask ourselves: What is it all about? A spirituality of reading in which we have reflected on the role that reading may play in the search for the true self? We have seen how reading has been our partner in our conversations with ourselves, our interiority; how it may have brought us to new ways of thinking and being, to conversions; how it meets our desires for intimacy. But finally, what is it all about?

It took me the writing of this entire book to discover that I think it is about love. That little word—*eros, caritas, agape*. That little spark, the trace in us of the Transcendent Other, who loves all creation, and who calls us to ever greater self-transcending love for and communion with all. Our reading, as it displays the whole world to us for our cherishing, may be a kind of *Contemplatio ad Amorem*, the concluding meditation in Ignatius's Spiritual Exercises, which calls us to find the love of God for us in all things, and all things in the God of love.

And maybe, when we have put down the book we are reading, we will have taken one more step toward finding our true selves, "God in you as you," the God who is love (1 John 4:8). In a 1997 lecture, "The Human Condition," at the Harvard Divinity School, Cistercian monk Thomas Keating concluded his remarks with this extraordinary statement: "If we have not experienced ourselves as unconditional love, then we have more work to do, because that is who we really are." Reading helps us, helps me, to love, "to be in love *in an unrestricted fashion*" (italics mine), Bernard Lonergan's definition of religious conversion, religious love. Reading helps me to be my true self, the self that sees the world, others, myself, God, with the faith that he calls "the eye of love."

EPILOGUE

"Give Beauty Back": An Apologia

I WALK DOWN to the beach this early October afternoon to see if the tide is right for a swim. Two swans, accustomed to being fed there, come waddling toward me on their splayed feet. I hold out my hands to show them I have no food. They stop, fold their legs beneath themselves, and tuck their orange beaks under their wings, perfectly symmetrical. On the weather-worn raft beached by the outgoing tide (too low for swimming), a cormorant holds its gray-black serrated wings stretched at full span, unmoving against the blue sky. I lie down, a piece of driftwood under my head, and feel the warmth of the sand through my jeans and shirt. Out of the breeze the sun is hot. What am I doing? Nothing. Enjoying the sun, gazing at the white swans, the black cormorant, the tranquil bay, the wide sky.

"In the beginning was the Word. . . . All things came into being through [the Word]" (John 1:1, 3)—the swans, the cormorant, the bay, the sky, creatures all, including me, gazing, savoring, praising, if only implicitly. I think about reading and writing, the human words that strive to mirror all of creation, making us see what is there to be seen, and in Hopkins's phrase, giving "beauty back" to the Creator. What have I been doing in the thousands of hours that I have spent reading but that? Giving beauty back, a terrible beauty sometimes, not all sweetness and light, but beautiful because true. "Full of grace and truth" (John 1:14), like the Word, these human words, too, have been grace for me, and like the Word, they have brought me into being, making me who I am in countless ways.

And what am I doing now, writing? How can I justify spending all this time putting words on paper? Shouldn't I be working in a soup kitchen, dealing somehow directly with the poor, the homeless, the sick, the uneducated, the imprisoned, with issues of peace and justice? These questions haunt me. I suspect that some of my sisters, working hard on the front lines as they are, have the same questions in regard to me.

In my perplexity I give myself various answers. I appeal to the doctrine of the church as the Mystical Body of Christ: they—all involved in these good works—are doing them on my behalf, and I am doing my work on theirs. "God arranged the members in the body, each one of them, as he chose. As it is, there are many members, yet one body. The eye cannot say to the hand, 'I have no need of you,' nor again the head to the feet, 'I have no need of you'" (1 Corinthians 12:20ff). I imagine that contemplative nuns and monks might have the same questions that I do about the worth of their lives; it takes a lot of faith in a pragmatic culture like ours and in the face of the world's ills to "do nothing" but pray.

It takes faith to believe in the power of the written word for good. It takes hope to hold that a work well made is its own excuse for being, all the while hoping, too, that those who have so much less than I find moments in which they know that life is more than mere survival, moments in which they find beauty, and "give beauty back" to the Creator in praise and thanksgiving.

In the end, it comes down to the swans, their beaks tucked beneath their wings, the cormorant, motionless, its wings outstretched—who knows why? You do what you were made to do. Some of us were made to read and write. Thanks be to God.

RECOMMENDED READING

Below is a short list of works and authors I admire, many not mentioned before in this book because, for one reason or another, they didn't fit into its schema. Among others, they have influenced me, instructed me, surprised me, given me pleasure. I offer my comments on them, loosely organized in different categories, hoping that if you haven't yet read them, you might be enticed to do so; and that if you have, you might experience a moment of "book kinship"; or that you be encouraged to make your own list from notable omissions of mine, or to disagree with the very personal opinions I offer. When I do cite a work named in the book, it is because I can't resist the opportunity to say something more about an old favorite.

Fiction

JAMES AGEE, *A Death in the Family,* posthumous Pulitzer Prize winner in 1957. A deeply human treatment of death. In it is the most masterful, accurate description of the kind of hilarity that can overtake us in the midst of grief—those two powerful emotions existing, inexplicably, side by side in our hearts.

A.S. BYATT'S *Possession,* which manages to combine a romance, a literary mystery story, some wonderful nineteenth-century poetry of her own composing, and gentle spoofs of the stuff of traditional literary scholarship and hilarious takeoffs on the jargon of pomo lit crit: e.g., a paper on "The Potent Castrato: The Phallogocentric Structuration of Balzac's Hermaphrodite Hero/ines."

WILLA CATHER, *My Ántonia.* I intend to reread this book. My memory of it is as being lucid, beautiful, whole, calm. I read it before and liked it more than *Death Comes to the Archbishop,* generally acknowledged to be Cather's masterpiece. But since we are not always our "best reader" selves, the fault in this appreciation may be mine.

MARGARET DRABBLE'S novels received critical acclaim in the seventies, and my friends in Cambridge and I loved them. Since the novels, she has written a biography of Arnold Bennett and devoted herself to scholarly and editorial work. (Drabble is the younger sister of Byatt, who didn't appear on my screen until decades later—and who was talking about her latest book, *A Whistling Woman*, on public radio at lunchtime yesterday.)

GEORGE ELIOT'S *Middlemarch*. This is one of those books for which contemporary readers may not have an appetite. Let me urge you to give it a try and to be patient with its rather formal prose. Both personal and social life are so closely and wisely observed, human nature so generously interpreted. I found myself challenged by the author's asides to be less judgmental, more understanding of her characters than I was inclined to be, an instance of a book accurately "reading" me and then instructing me.

SHUSAKU ENDO, *Silence*. In this somber little book, Endo, Japanese and a Roman Catholic, explores the terrible moral/ religious choice confronting his seventeenth-century

Portuguese missionary protagonist: whether to adhere to his Christian faith or to save the lives of others by publicly denouncing the Christ in whom he believes.

GABRIEL GARCÍA MÁRQUEZ, Nobel Prize winner in 1982. *One Hundred Years of Solitude* is a big book with big themes—not heavy, however, but full of life, exuberant. His "magic realism" works for me in a way that fantasy— e.g., C. S. LEWIS's *The Chronicles of Narnia*—usually doesn't. Another exception in the fantasy realm is URSULA LE GUIN's thought-provoking imaginative treatment of gender/sexuality in *The Left Hand of Darkness*.

NADINE GORDIMER. Better than anyone, in my opinion, Gordimer brings home the truth, not that the personal is political, as feminists have it, but that the political is personal. In *The House Gun*, a middle-aged white professional husband and wife wait to hear whether their only son will receive the death penalty for a murder he admits to. Imagine how you would feel about the death penalty if your son were on death row; everyone on death row now is someone's son—or daughter. The political is personal. (From the high-cheekboned, full-face book jacket photographs of her, I always imagined Gordimer to be a tall, rangy woman. Last fall, I went to a reading she gave at the 92nd Street Y.

She is tiny, her face delicate. I must have thought one had
to be big to tackle the tough issues she takes on. . . .)

MAUREEN HOWARD. A portrait of her on the cover of the
July 1, 2001, *New York Times Book Review,* the review of *Big
as Life* titled "Up from Bridgeport": Bridgeport vindicated!
Reviewer John Leonard said, "Why Howard isn't cher-
ished more is mystifying. It's as if, while nobody watched,
Mary McCarthy had grown up to be Nadine Gordimer [I
find her more like Byatt], getting smarter, going deeper,
writing better than ever before. . . ." I knew Howard as a
teenager; we both frequented Restmore, the Irish Catholic
beach club in Fairfield, and I have met her and spoken with
her a few times in these later years. She wouldn't, I'm sure,
characterize herself as a "religious" writer, but religious/
liturgical themes and metaphors abound in her books. Full
of "thisness"—almanacs, natural history—the books dis-
play a sacramental Catholic/catholic imagination.

P. D. JAMES: For those who want good writing, complex
characterization, and moral heft in their mystery stories.
Likewise, JOHN LE CARRÉ, for even "darker" spy stories.

JAMES JOYCE: the novel *A Portrait of the Artist as a
Young Man* and the short story collection *Dubliners.* I

found myself ethnically at home in these books, much less daunting than *Ulysses*.

DAVID LODGE: *Small World* and *Thinks*. Having written critical works on literary theory and the role of language in literature, Lodge, an Englishman, light-handedly satirizes (not without serious intent) academia, its mores, morals, and literary fashions and fads in these two novels that are fun to read.

BRIAN MOORE, *Black Robe*. This piercing novel dispelled any romantic notions I had about the life of early missionaries in the new world. Its hero is a devout young French missionary in seventeenth-century Canada, and it describes the brutality he encountered there on every level. It was especially meaningful to me because Ursulines were the first nuns to come to North America, arriving in Canada in 1639. I never before realized how harsh their life must have been.

ALICE MUNRO. Set in southwestern Ontario, Munro's stories deal with the questions of identity, personal relationships, passion, and commitment that confront her female characters. I'm looking forward to reading her latest collection, *Hateship, Friendship, Loveship, Marriage*.

PATRICK O'BRIAN'S *Master and Commander* and *The Far Side of the World* have been adapted for a film starring Russell Crowe as Captain Aubrey. If you haven't read O'Brian's historical novels about life aboard a British frigate during the Napoleonic wars, these books, the tenth and the first in the Aubrey/Maturin series, might be a good place to begin. O'Brian leads us into a world different from ours— a whole world in its political, economic, social, religious, intellectual, and aesthetic dimensions. We're intrigued, we learn; and yet we recognize and savor what is familiar in all of this—human nature as it is depicted by the author in all its wonderful vagaries.

WALKER PERCY: *The Moviegoer, The Last Gentleman, Love in the Ruins, Lancelot, The Thanatos Syndrome,* profound (and sometimes very funny) novels about the spiritual malaise of late-twentieth-century American culture.

ANNA QUINDLEN, *One True Thing.* I wrote to Quindlen after reading this book and told her I thought it was "true," in the sense that we mean when we say a singer's pitch is true. The scene I vividly remember: the protagonist/ daughter, with the most complex mix of emotions, giving her cancer-ridden mother a bath.

Short Pieces That Have Made Me Laugh

Most of STEVE MARTIN in *The New Yorker*'s "Shouts & Murmurs" section. Also in *The New Yorker*, JAMIE MALANOWSKI'S 1995 musings on "character" as the most important quality that Colin Powell would bring to a number of hypothetical positions. Both writers, with unimaginable imaginative leaps, avoid the trap of repeating the same joke over and over, which is what I find in a lot of "Shouts & Murmurs" features. And in WOODY ALLEN'S *Without Feathers*, the piece titled "If the Impressionists Had Been Dentists," which gives us van Gogh writing to his brother Theo about teeth! Even though I can't remember a single line, I laugh here at the computer just thinking about it.

Nonfiction

ANNIE DILLARD: *Pilgrim at Tinker's Creek,* 1974 Pulitzer Prize winner, and *Holy the Firm*. Quirky, written with style and bite, they ask the hard theological/spiritual questions about violence, death, and decay in nature, including human nature.

PAULO FREIRE, *Pedagogy of the Oppressed.* This book was like a Bible for some of us in the sixties. Coming out of the base community movement in Brazil, it proposed a method for educating the poor, teaching them to read and decode the dominant culture so as not to be coopted by it.

ALBERTO MANGUEL'S *A History of Reading.* Full of information about all facets of reading, the book is as well a personal essay by someone who loves books.

And even if you don't read all of HERMIONE LEE's grand biography of Virginia Woolf, do peruse the chapter called "Reading." It is both insightful and delightful.

SR. HELEN PREJEAN'S clearly and powerfully written *Dead Man Walking,* about her ministry to men on death row and the families of their victims, is the only book by a nun that I know of reviewed by *The New York Review of Books.* (I once heard Sr. Helen speak. With her charming southern accent and droll humor, she made mention of a man "sittin' on his li'l fanny" outside a courtroom or something. Do you think that a nun from the Northeast corridor, like me, could get away with saying anything like that? Accent excepted, Susan Sarandon's portrayal of Sister Helen in the film gave, in my opinion, an accurate picture of many contemporary American sisters.)

E. F. SCHUMACHER, *Small Is Beautiful: A Study of Economics As If People Mattered*, published in 1973 and named in the New York Public Library's Books of the Century. Read at least the introduction to this book, and, if you feel the way I do about the present state of the world, look back with sadness at "the road not taken."

DAVA SOBEL: *Longitude* and *Galileo's Daughter*. The first is a small, elegant book that tells the story of another of those marvelous, crucially important developments—like the alphabet—that we take for granted: in this case, the measuring and marking of longitude on a map. Sobel teaches us the relevant science and at the same time recounts the all-too-human tale of the prejudice, political maneuvering, and neglect that its "hero" had to contend with. *Galileo's Daughter: A Historical Memoir of Science, Faith, and Love* chronicles the astonishing scientific accomplishments of this great man, his suffering at the hands of church authorities, and, at the same time, celebrates the touching relationship that he maintained with his illegitimate daughter, a cloistered nun. (There were no photos of the author on the book jackets, but I saw her on public television, a handsome, mature woman. I had previously discovered, by chance, that she—so learned, such a wonderful writer—is also an accomplished amateur ballroom dancer. Does that delight you? It delights me—personal "thisness.")

Biography and Autobiography

JAMES MCBRIDE, *The Color of Water*. Ingeniously structured in alternating chapters that give us the mother's history and point of view in her own voice and that of her son as he explores the mystery of his mother's identity. The mystery is this: She's white, Jewish, and the widow of a black preacher with whom she cofounded a black church. Her son is black, and as a child, he can't figure out why his mother looks different from the other women in the neighborhood. He asks her at one point, "What color is God?" She answers, "The color of water."

DAVID MCCULLOUGH'S *John Adams*, which I can't recommend highly enough, is a hefty book, hard to hold and read in bed, but, besides teaching me the American history I never learned in school, it made me appreciate the originality and value of the American experiment in democratic government. I would add McCullough's Pulitzer Prize–

winning *Truman*. Two books about two very different Americans, each great in his own way.

IDA GOERRES, *The Hidden Face*. If you have never read the life of a saint, start here and be surprised. And, if you have vague, sweetness-and-light ideas about "the Little Flower," as St. Thérèse of Lisieux is known among devotees, ditto. You'll find steely resolve and darkness aplenty.

DOROTHY DAY (1897–1980) has been mentioned as a candidate for canonization in the Roman Catholic Church; you couldn't find someone whose life was more outwardly different from Thérèse's if you tried. Day, well known to Catholic activists, was a writer, a journalist (Mike Bloy thought she wrote the best prose in America), a friend of Eugene O'Neill and company, a radical and a pacifist, who spent time in jail more than once for protesting government policy; she underwent an abortion in her twenties, and gave birth to a daughter in a common-law marriage. In 1933, six years after her conversion to Catholicism at age thirty, she and French-born Peter Maurin began publishing a monthly newspaper, *The Catholic Worker*, still sold for a penny an issue, and founded the Catholic Worker Houses of Hospitality for the homeless and hungry. JIM

FOREST'S *Love Is the Measure: A Biography of Dorothy Day* offers a fine little introduction to her. In *The Long Loneliness,* Day tells her own story; her *On Pilgrimage* records her journeys and reflections over the course of a year.

DIANNA ORTIZ, *The Blindfold's Eyes: My Journey from Torture to Truth*. I haven't yet read this book by a beautiful American Ursuline decades younger than I. Just published, it is an account of her 1989 rape and torture in Guatemala, and of the part the U.S. government played in the politics of the country at the time, and in her case in particular. Even though I don't know Dianna, who is a member of a different branch of Ursulines, I expect this to be a book like an ax.

Spiritual Reading and Theology

For those specifically interested in prayer, meditation, and contemplation, I would mention two Roman Catholics whose books might now be considered "classics": Irish Jesuit WILLIAM JOHNSTON, who spent many years in Japan, and American Cistercian THOMAS KEATING.

BEATRICE BRUTEAU is less well known, even among Catholics. In *What We Can Learn from the East*, "The Immaculate Conception: Our Original Face," an essay that first appeared in *Cross Currents*, offers a good example of the kind of work that Bruteau, a philosopher, does. She carefully interprets the Catholic dogma that Mary was conceived without original sin as an archetype, a revelation about *all* of us, not just the mother of Jesus. She then aligns this interpretation with the Far Eastern truth of our Original Face, "the face we had before our parents were born"—that is, untouched by what the East calls illusion and the West calls sin.

Russian Orthodox Archbishop ANTHONY BLOOM's *Beginning to Pray* is only seventy-five pages long. The cosmopolitan author was an army surgeon, a French Resistance fighter, a monk, and a priest before being consecrated bishop in England. The book, based on talks the author gave to people who had never prayed before, is bracingly honest and down-to-earth, serving up both comforting and uncomfortable truths about ourselves, our prayers, and the Being who is worthy to be called God. Unsentimental, it is full of deep feeling, a remarkable book to which I have returned many times over the years.

KATHLEEN NORRIS: *Dakota: A Spiritual Geography, The Cloister Walk*, and *Amazing Grace: A Vocabulary of Faith*. Norris, a published poet, a Protestant, and a Benedictine oblate (lay associate), translates monastic spirituality into the everyday stuff of her own sometimes chaotic life in a fascinating and helpful way.

WILLIAM STRINGFELLOW, *An Ethic for Christians and Other Aliens in a Strange Land*, the author's "biblical politics," in which he reads America as Babylon, "its institutions, systems, ideologies, and other political and social power as principalities—militant, aggressive, and immensely influential creatures." Another cautionary book gone unheeded. (Stringfellow was a member of the Church Society board, an Episcopalian, and a lawyer. He defended the first women "illicitly" ordained in the Episcopal church; and Jesuit Dan Berrigan, wanted by the FBI for his protests against the war in Vietnam, was captured by them on Stringfellow's property.)

For the Theologically Minded

ELIZABETH JOHNSON, *She Who Is: The Mystery of God in Feminist Theological Discourse*. "As perhaps the best book

of feminist theology to date, [it] is at once thoroughly orthodox, grounded in classical Christian thought, liberat-
ingly contemporary, and rooted in Women's experience,"
said *Library Journal*. Although Johnson's language is theologically accurate, she writes clearly and freshly, beautifully even. She makes the case, as the title indicates, for
speaking of God—"I am who I am" (Exodus 3:14)—in
feminine language and images, thus calling into question
the prevailing structures of patriarchy, the "divine right"
of men.

BERNARD LONERGAN, *Method in Theology*. I have gleaned
my knowledge of Lonergan from friends who know more
about his work than I do and from this book. It is not an
easy read, not because it is obscure, but because Lonergan
writes so precisely and compactly. Jesuit TAD DUNNE'S
Lonergan: Spirituality: Toward a Spiritual Integration offers
an accessible introduction to the master's thought. Please
note that the book you are reading began with a reflection
on Lonergan's notion of unrestricted questioning and
ended with "being in love in an unrestricted fashion"—the
answer to all our questioning, questing.

INDEX

PERMISSIONS